ONE LOVE

ONE LOVE
Life with Bob Marley & the Wailers
Words and Photographs by Lee Jaffe
Introduction and Interview by Roger Steffens
Design by Geoff Gans

W.W. Norton & Company
New York • London

Printed in Italy
First Edition

The text of this book is composed in AG Oldface Regular
With the display set in Officina Sans Italic
Composition by Geoff Gans
Manufacturing by Mondadori Printing, Verona
Book design and photo editing/retouching by Geoff Gans (of Culver City)
Editor and Production Manager: James Mairs

Library of Congress Cataloging-in-Publication Data
Jaffe, Lee, 1950 -
One Love: Life with Bob Marley and the Wailers/ by Lee Jaffe.
p.cm.
ISBN: 0-393-05143-9 (cloth)
ISBN: 0-393-32368-4 (pbk)
Marley, Bob - Pictorial Works. 2. Wailers (Reggae group) - Pictorial works. I.
Title.
ML420.M3313 J34 2003
782.421646'092--dc21
[B]

2002067090

W. W. Norton & Company, 500 Fifth Avenue, New York, NY 10110
www.wwnorton.com

W. W. Norton & Company Ltd., Castle House, 75/76 Wells Street,
London, WIT 3QT

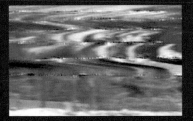

About the designer:

GEOFF GANS (unpublished autobiography) An accomplished designer, the (long) time L.A. resident, a seasoned veteran of the music industry and five-time Grammy Nominee for his art direction of boxed sets, is half of Varèse-Sarabande Records, Rhino Records, Atlantic Records, DIW of the Village, Restless and Enigma. His extensive client list includes Atlantic Records, Capitol, A&M, Rhino and Restless, among others. An accomplished artist in his own right, Gans created the graphic design work for the collected Bob Dylan in the mid-90s, and since then he has been Dylan's personal art director, responsible for everything from his album covers and tour posters to books that include Dylan's collected lyrics. A longtime fine art and graphic Gans currently resides in Culver City, CA from which his one-of-a-kind in constant demand work can be seen.

Table of Contents

When I first went to Jamaica and began my life with the Wailers the first person that Bob Marley introduced me to was Joe Higgs. Joe was Bob's mentor, the person who taught him to play guitar, the one who gave the Wailers their first lessons in harmonizing. So much tragedy has engulfed the Wailers, but perhaps more than any personal tragedy the circumstances of Joe's passing are symbolic of a greater one. Although the music has become so popular, generating tens of millions of dollars in sales year in and year out, the neighborhoods where the music was born, the sufferers and the children of sufferers who are the inspiration for the music have been unable to reap any benefits.

The Mighty Joe Higgs, whose music and teachings have permeated the globe, whose five albums received so much critical acclaim, died penniless at the age of fifty-nine in a welfare hospital in Los Angeles. I consider myself so blessed to have been his friend and student and to have been able to produce two of his albums and it is with great sadness that one we were working on was not completed. He had so much more to give.

It is to him that I dedicate this work.

— Lee Jaffe, Feb. 2002

"Forward"

The book you hold is the direct result of a chance meeting in a hotel room in New York in 1973 between the just-about-to-break reggae icon Bob Marley and Lee Jaffe, a precocious 22 year old artist and film-maker with a keenly tuned instinct for history. Pulling out his omnipresent harmonica, Jaffe began to jam with Marley on guitar, and an instant friendship blossomed. "Bob said, 'Why don't you come with us to Jamaica?'" recalls Jaffe three decades later from his base in Los Angeles, laughing. "And I never came back."

Indeed, his life has been inextricably involved with reggae music since then, as photographer, musician, writer and producer working with such island luminaries as Marley's original teacher, Joe Higgs, and the Wailing Souls (whom Higgs also mentored), as well as Barrington Levy.

For many years, whenever I would meet up with Jaffe along the reggae trail I would ask to interview him about the three years he ended up living with Bob Marley, Peter Tosh and Bunny Livinginston—the original Wailers. "We should do a book," he'd counter. Finally, in 1998, we agreed on a format. We would present images that he had taken between 1973 and 1976, the most crucial time in reggae's development, in a wide variety of formats: 4x5 transparencies, 35 mm color and black and white prints, polaroids, plus black and white (and later color) video. To these would be added the transcripts of our interviews, as Lee told his compelling story in his own articulate, off-the-cuff words. Several times I asked Lee to go home and make some notes about a subject I would like to discuss at the next session. When he began showing me the notes, meticulously observed sense paintings in a grammar that frequently introduced new words to this lifelong writer, I realized that they must be part of the final product as well. So the text you read is a complementary mixture of both, each further illuminating the other.

As for these amazing unpublished pictures herein, Lee reveals his commitment that "each person who made a significant contribution to the music I photographed is here." This unseen cream of three years of living with the legends is "about one third of everything I shot. I carried a camera almost everywhere, but I was discreet. I could tell when it was not a good time to be photographing. You look for the light or mood to be a certain way—or the situation to be relaxed enough or tense enough that the camera wouldn't be obtrusive. I felt like I was chronicling a very important epic culturally."

From hooking Marley up for a historic week long gig at the ultimate '70s artist hangout, Max's Kansas City, opening for Bruce Springsteen, to playing harmonica on the breakthrough *Natty Dread* album; and producing Peter Tosh's debut lp, *Legalize It*, for which he also shot the controversial cover—Jaffe was at the absolute nerve center of a mighty music machine at the moment it began to "mosh down the world" and help change it forever. Here, at last, is the deepest insider's account ever of those tumultuous days, in words and pictures that further cement Bob Marley's reputation as the "Artist of the Century," and bring new light onto the huge contributions of Bunny and Peter.

— Roger Steffens, July 2002

ROGER STEFFENS lectures internationally on the lives of Bob Marley and Peter Tosh. His Reggae Archives in L.A. are considered the world's largest collection of reggae recordings and memorabilia, and were on display for eight months in 2001 at the Queen Mary in Long Beach, CA. Co-founder of The Beat magazine and chairman since its inception in 1985 of the Reggae Grammy Committee, Steffens is also a photographer, producer, and actor, specializing in voice-overs. He can be heard narrating Oscar and Emmy-winning documentaries, as well as in movies like Forrest Gump, Wag the Dog and The American President. He has been a principal resources for several VH1 "Behind the Music" episodes, and is often interviewed in his role as reggae's most public American activist. He and Geoff Gans collaborated on the recent book The World of Reggae featuring Bob Marley: Treasures from Roger Steffens' Reggae Archives (Global Treasures, 2001). rasrojah@aol.com

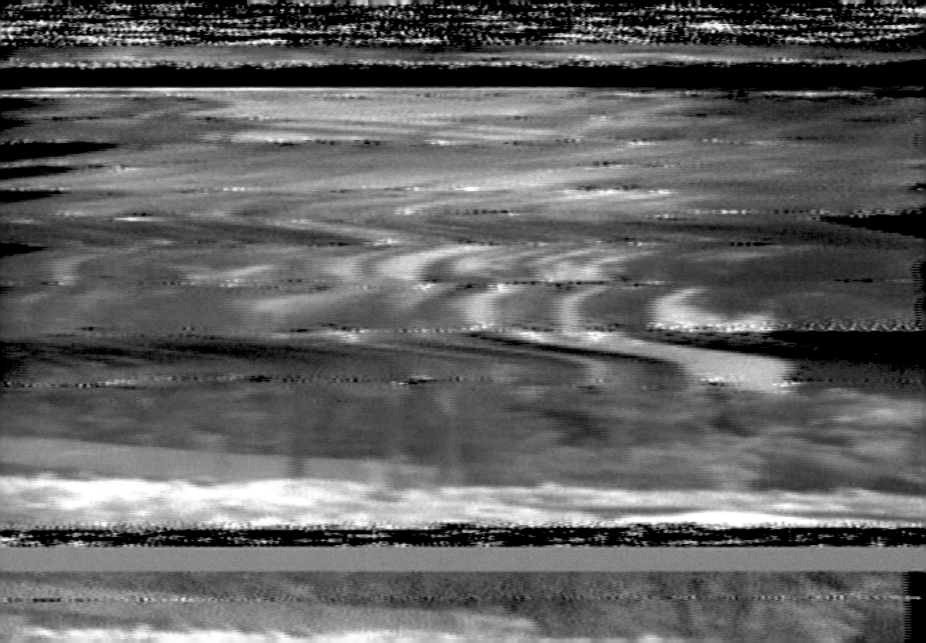

"ONE LOVE....
ONE HEART...LET'S
GET TOGETHER
AND FEEL
ALRIGHT."

— BOB MARLEY

Roger Steffens: How did you first meet Bob?

Lee Jaffe: The first time I met Bob was in January 1973, in New York City. It was at a hotel then called the Windsor, on Fifty-sixth Street and Sixth Avenue. I was visiting Jim Capaldi, the drummer and co-writer of songs for the group called Traffic. Traffic, one of the most popular bands in the world, both critically and commercially, had just broken up. One of the members was a junkie and couldn't perform anymore, and somewhere in the midst of an American tour, the group imploded. I went to visit Jim, whom I had met through the actress Esther Anderson in England. It was a typical early seventies rock and roll–type scene, with groupies running around the halls and various press and record company people. Bob Marley was in Jim's room, sitting in a corner of this big suite, very quiet, very shy. We just started talking. He told me he had finished an album for Island Records, *Catch a Fire*. He had a cassette of it that we listened to. I had just seen *The Harder They Come* in England the week before, so I was totally prepared. It was like the movie had just walked off the screen. And I was now face to face with the voice of a group whose music was the most revolutionary I had ever heard, who was both black and white and transcended race, whose music was both spiritually and socially conscious.

That was the beginning of a week that Bob and I spent together in New York. He had this look about him, a certain aura, a certain calmness, a certain stoicism amid all the rock and roll hubris. In it but not of it. But certainly not out of place. The album was completely contagious. I was very anxious to show off what I had found to all my artist and musician friends in New York. I was staying in a loft at 112 Greene Street, in SoHo, the center of the art world at that time. On the ground floor and in the basement was a gallery that was run communally by artists. Now it's Greene Street Recording Studios, where some classic hip-hop has been recorded. I was in the first show at this gallery in 1970, and the great thing about it was that it wasn't a gallery. The floors were all wood and corroded. In the basement, Gordon Matta-Clarke, one of the great sculptors of the twentieth century, son of the surrealist painter Matta, had "recycled" all these glass bottles. It was the first time I'd ever heard the word "recycle." The concept didn't exist until then. It was a mound of empty bottles and a pile of dirt. He cut a hole in the ceiling that led to the first floor of the gallery, and he set up some lights in the basement and was able to make a rose grow out of the dirt and garbage and recycled bottles. Gordon was amazing. He created an aesthetics of garbage. For other sculptures, he went to Staten Island dumps to create with bulldozers. He had a way of speaking about his art that was as crucial as seeing it. For as powerful as it was visually, Gordon would never allow it to leave the realm of social critique and revolutionary reformation. He brought a humanistic fire to the art world in a way the Wailers brought it to popular music. Gordon was of Chilean descent, and I was preparing a film in New York with a cast and crew ready to leave for Chile, where that week our Chilean co-producer had "disappeared" in the CIA-backed coup that overthrew Salvador Allende, the head of the longest-living democracy in South America. The inspiration for the movie had come from tales of a walking trip through the Andes that Gordon had made with Jeffrey Lew, the artist who owned the 112 Greene Street building.

It was at that time, too, that I met Dickie Jobson, then Bob's manager. Dickie was the best friend of Chris Blackwell, the owner of Island Records, the label that had recently signed the Wailers. Dickie was a fellow Jamaican and Chris's partner in various real estate ventures on the island. Dickie had come to New York with Bob to buy equipment for the band. I went with them to Manny's on Forty-eighth Street, where every musician up to the biggest rock stars would go to buy equipment. I helped them pick out their gear and deal with all the salesmen.

I took Bob around to visit musician friends. He'd play guitar, I'd play harmonica. The only thing that came close to my friends' reaction to his album was their reaction to Jimi Hendrix's first album in '67.

The fog was a dense silver blue, chilling the late October night. Breath, a soft glow, like young dragons delighting in the newness of the universe. We boarded the steel gray buick station wagon for the slow, deliberate and interminable trek through the San Francisco streets, cautious and confident (the promoter informing us he expected a near full house), the sound check earlier having gone well in the expansive ballroom with its competent and sympathetic engineer helming a real decent sound system at a club of around 800 capacity called The Matrix. I pulled around the rear of the venue and we unfolded out. I grabbed Bob's guitar from the back, feeling that I was part of the group whose power was eternal, ordained so by Jah. I had yet to record a note with them, and it would be more than a year before I would get my stage initiation and become a true Wailer. There was a club worker at the back entrance who escorted us through a narrow hallway. Walls were stickered and postered with stuff like "Moby Grape" and "Country Joe And The Fish" – lingering psychdelia just to let us know where we were. We were led into a shabby but posh dressing room with a giant comfy couch, big velvet chairs(somewhat tattered) and a massive table harboring a throne of tropical fruits. Obviously someone had taken care to make us feel wanted. People started emerging - kind strangers with gifts of various herb to smoke - some awkward, others too familiar, but everyone with the charged air of anticipation, feeling that this was more than just a new hot group that was gonna play. The dressing room filled with sweet and pungent clouds. The club was filling. I moved to check the engineer at the mixing board which was three-quarters back into the room and centered with the stage. I then slipped back through the crowd to the dressing room and helped Bob write out a song list and then,determined and focused, The Wailers filed onto the stage. The lights were dimmed..shouts from the mostly white crowd, "Rastaman, Dreadlocks..." the sounds of "Rastaman Chant" with Nyabingi drums setting the transcendental mood...the crowd screaming as it finished and segued into "Lively Up Yourself". I stood at the board as the engineer pulled up the bass and, as the pace began to throb, the crowd grew more and more ecstatic. Bob was dancing actively and with more agility than i'd ever seen him with on the football field. Into a second encore, which was "Slave Driver", he made and unforgettable move, bending backward so far as to almost touch the the floor. I couldn't believe that he didn't fall, but somehow, miraculously, he pulled himself up, and with his right arm swinging, his hand came down on a chord with perfect timing as he sang, "slave driver, you're gonna get burned". The next morning we were packing to leave the motel. I ran out to get the paper hoping for a review. The San Francisco Chronicle had a headline for the entertainment section that read: "Apocalyptic - THE WAILERS at the Matrix"

The ice crackled under my feet. The wind taunted my breath. If I had known, really, what a Rastaman was, I would have thought this was no place for a Rastaman. We were cruel weather's toys, hunched in our coats, begging for Mother Nature's forgiveness. But we were on a mission. A mission that, for the years we sparred, was interminable, relentless, intractable—the search for the better herb.

I pierced the night air with a high-pitched wail to let Bob know I was a sufferer too, and it was all he could do not to double over laughing as we picked up the pace along Central Park West, trying not to lose our balance on the salted-slick sidewalk, coming down Eighty-fifth Street, to where my friend Brew, a main distributor of the better strains of Colombian golds and reds, kept a stash house.

Normally only Brew's dispatcher, the Dile, was ever allowed there. He accepted deliveries of bales enclosed in innocuous cardboard boxes to the brownstone apartment, and in turn distributed them to a half-

like The Scene and Salvation, and helped us buy drugs, which helped us pick up more girls.

When I was done with college, I went off to Brazil, and Brew continued his life in the herb trade, eventually convincing his brother to quit his lucrative Wall Street job to come help him turn his successful pot dealing into a real business. Now we were together escorting the new signee to the label of Traffic and Cat Stevens, eager to impress this third world advocate of herbs and revolution.

The pale din of headlights bobbing, a cab scowling around a corner, a beggar in sundry rags, wheeling a shopping cart overflowing with all his worldly possessions, coughed, floated among the newly floating flakes of snow glowing in the lamplight, teetered on the verge of madness, and disappeared from consciousness as we bounded up the brownstone stairs toward the ethereal cathedral of cannabis.

Was I proud. My old buddy made good. Bale upon bale of crocus-sacked mystical foliage, which in turn were clear plastic—wrapped

dozen dealers scattered through the city. But I was a trusted exception.

I had met Brew through his brother the Fox in the late sixties. I went to college with him at Penn State, where I had been one of the students mainly responsible for elevating the consciousness of a significant portion of the student body by turning them on to various (what were then exotic) controlled substances. We had hung out a lot in New York during our breaks from school; he, an aspiring artist like me, stayed at his parents' swanky Upper East Side apartment, which had a leopard-skin pattern velvet couch and a perfect view of the East River and the Fifty-ninth Street Bridge. His parents were living mostly in Florida. I'd often stay over there, and we'd spend our time getting high, tripping, and having sex with as many girls as possible. We did our first pot deals together. We'd scrape together enough money to buy a pound, and then sell ounces and half-ounces. The proceeds got us into concerts at the Fillmore East, and clubs

and sealed, numbered and graded A or AA, with weights 22.5, 26.3 magic markered on the see-through outer covering. I looked into Bob's deep mischievous eyes. He glared in return... A pause like a pause between Aston "Family Man" Barrett's bass notes.... "You t'ink you somethin', Lee Jaffe...." Then laughter volcanoing, lyrical, the sounds beading off each other, luminous. Brew shook his head and resisted a smile. He liked to think of himself as hard. He was taking kung fu and had grown a short, scruffy beard to disguise his baby face. I had turned him on to an advance copy of Catch A Fire, and he had all the lyrics of the songs memorized in just a few days. "Everytime I hear the crack of a whip, my blood run cold. I remember on a slave ship how they brutalized our very soul." Mimicking Bob's accent. Then, in falsetto, "Catch a fire," as he whipped a switchblade from his jeans pocket and, with the shimmering blade, motioned for us to follow him to the back room of the long cavernous apartment.

The floor was covered with Afghan and Indian rugs and pillows, and in the dim transitory light he opened a Moroccan-looking chest containing several small bricks of bud and, lifting one, punctiliously carving an opening in the herbal sheath with the lacerating weapon, pulled out a handful of black, well-defined sticky and, holding it up face-high for us to whiff and contemplate, declared, "Cheeba."

The sound resonated clear through to the mountains and sequestered valleys of Cartagena. Peasants plying the fields, gathering the cured stalks hanging upside down in the steamy afternoon haze. I imagined hundreds with Juan Valdez hats and tiny scissors, clipping the buds off the thick, tough, tacky branches, soft-pressing them into bales, meandering on donkeys down craggy hillsides to meet ancient generic trucks, the grizzled drivers with machine guns waiting for the chance to deliver the sweet and pungent cargo to a trawler of undetermined origin, parked Federale-protected in the azure-glistening Caribbean harbor.

Then, the overlong voyage around the Caribbean into the green Atlantic to avoid DEA detection, with designated gringo on board, swinging back in toward the Florida Keys to rendezvous with Miami-Cuban cigarette boats too swift for the Coast Guard to follow, the state-of-the-art speedboats cutting razor-thin wakes in the semi-tropical moonlight, meeting waiting vans ready to scurry up the perilous one-road causeway through the Keys to a Homestead warehouse south of Miami where my other college friend, Robbie, and his harmonica-playing Italian partner, Johnny B., from South Plainfield, New Jersey, would come to sort through their allotment, paying extra to Stone and Jonni (ultimately a Wailers fan), their Cuban connections, for the chance to pick the best to send in car trunks and false-backed U-Hauls up the coast to the first city.

I had some zigzags and offered them around. Brew beamed, being the Man, and we broke up buds on a large, lavishly engraved silver tray. He sensed Bob's consternation and jumped in, "It's cool, mon. I rent this place from my brethren and he's the only other tenant in the building. Everything's safe here, mon." It was the beginning of white Americans talking like Jamaicans. I thought, laughing to and at myself, damn, what a trendsetter I am. Bob rolled such a giant spliff it shocked even Brew. He blurted, "This herb very very strong, mon," as if to say, no need for such exaggeration. But what Brew didn't know was that that was just a normal-sized joint for the Rastaman.

Bob lit the spliff, and gave Brew a sly, discerning smile. He took some short quick tokes, fanning the fire, before taking a long, deep draw, the smoke disappearing, reappearing, filling the beclouded room. Brew stopped trying to act unimpressed. We were both bug-eyed. I had taken hundreds of acid trips, peyote, psilocibin, I had been smoking since I was fifteen and was now twenty-two, but I knew as my jaw dropped I was entering a new world. The world of The Most High. It was not just the size of the spliff but the whole way that Bob

approached it—with such reverence, such respect. For Brew it was a path toward a new Mercedes and Rolex watches, and boosting his ego. For me it was a way to help reveal mystical truths. But for Bob it was something more. A way to connect and live in harmony with his Otherness. A gateway to a universe where words and music flowed in clear unpolluted celestial streams, sometimes raging, sometimes lazily weaving through the palm-tree-pillared rainbow kingdom of Jah, where sun and rain mixed in tranquil bliss and King David played upon his harp.

RS: Who else did Bob encounter during that first week you knew each other?

LJ: On any given day while I was at Jeffrey Lew's on Greene Street, artists like Robert Rauschenberg and Vito Acconci, composers like Phillip Glass and Steve Reich, and rock stars like Lou Reed would stop by the Gallery. Staying with me were a number of French movie stars who were going to be in my movie, including Maria Schneider, Jean-Pierre Kalfon, and the jamaican actress Esther Anderson, who had just starred in a big-budget Hollywood movie with Sidney Poitier; she was in one movie after the next, she was a movie star whose career was really taking off.

RS: What was the name of that film?

LJ: Warm December. And she was in another film at that time called *The*

Chris Blackwell on board the DC3 he rented to go island-hopping with friends between Jamaica and Trinidad. Carnival time, winter 1973. Chris had his own pilot, and I knew when I stepped on board that plane that I had entered a realm previously foreign to me, the world of rock and roll royalty. I remember Chris telling me, "You know you're doing well when you're making money when you sleep." I had never met someone with such a calm demeanor. Later I heard people in the music business refer to him as "the baby-face killer." He was, and I'm sure still is, a charming and gracious host.

I could taste the sugar cane in the air

Touchables; she was happening. Jeffrey's loft was enormous. It was the beginning of artists moving into SoHo. His was a turn-of-the-century industrial building with round pillars running through it and redone, polished wood floors, in contrast to the anti-gallery below.

It occurred to me from time to time that week that this was a world that was almost as foreign to Bob's experience as his music was to mine. But the fact that my artist friends embraced the Wailers' record was not so strange—great music is universal. This was a world where people were traveling often to distant places: Jeffrey and the artist Gordon Matta-Clarke to the Andes, the sculptor Alan Saret had just returned from India, I had been to Brazil. There was a kind of undercurrent of anthropological democracy in which there was a conscious attempt to deconstruct the object and have art exist strictly in the realm of ideas for both aesthetic and political reasons. Their seeing the action of creating an object to be produced, bought, and sold in a capitalist realm as being the most reactionary action one can take as an artist. However, music was seen as being safe from this trap, and therefore Bob walking into this world where being a poet and musician was regarded at first sight without suspicion made it easy for him to be comfortable in my world from the start. For that week that we were together, the *Catch A Fire* album became the soundtrack for what was at that time the center of the art world.

Gordon and his girlfriend had the first restaurant in SoHo, called Food. It was where the Mercer Hotel is now. At various times they would have different artists come in and be the

chef. Bob and I went there one night and had Cajun food from a menu authored by artist Kieth Sonnier.

Meantime, my French cast and crew was getting impatient. Everyone had busy schedules and had carved out just two to three weeks to devote to this project. The time to leave for Chile was getting near, with an upheaval going on there, and the Chilean part of the production not to be found. Chris Blackwell had rented a DC-3, which was waiting in Jamaica for a trip to Trinidad for Carnival. He had invited a bunch of friends, including Jim Capaldi and Esther Anderson, and Esther suggested to Chris that he invite Bob and me. With nowhere to go, it sounded like a great idea. I convinced Liani, a Brazilian girlfriend who was about to leave for Rio, to come to Jamaica with me, as it was on the way. Liani was the daughter of the owner of TV Globo, the largest TV station in Brazil. She was tall and thin, with exquisite olive skin and black eyes, long, straight black hair, an incredible beauty, and she was the sister of Maria Do Rosario, a TV and movie star, who was married to Neville D'Almeida, a radical underground filmmaker who was exiled to England by the military government. Liani and Maria used to act in Neville's films.

We arrived in Kingston at night. Dickie Jobson picked us up. As we drove through the city, I could taste the sugar cane in the air.

RS: Where did you go when you arrived?

LJ: We went to an incredible place in the hills above Kingston. Dickie Jobson had this house that was halfway up Strawberry Hill. And because I was traveling with Liani, who looked part Indian, I felt less foreign. Dickie parked us in a bedroom with a waterfall that seemed like it was going through the room. It was dreamlike, it was spectacular, it was some sort of paradise. And it was night, couldn't see anything, but it was all so lush, moving from this insipid aura, coming in from the airport, I felt the harbors and the refineries, the pollution, and this whole legacy of slavery, and then transcending into paradise. It was this intense dichotomy you always feel in Jamaica, living in heaven and living in hell at the same time. This is a Bob song I like a lot.

RS: Yeah, "Time Will Tell." ["Think you're in heaven but you're living in Hell."] So what happened in the morning when you woke up and saw your surroundings? Did you have a view of the city?

LJ: It was in the mountains, nestled in a canyon, and I felt like I was in the Garden of Eden.

RS: You didn't see any slums, any poverty?

LJ: No, no, no. It was spectacular.

RS: So it was Jim Capaldi from Traffic who went with you to Carnival, and Bob and Esther, Chris Blackwell, you—who else?

LJ: Someone named Abe Somers and his then wife, whose name was Phyllis. He's an American entertainment attorney. And Dickie Jobson.

RS: So how long were you actually in Jamaica before you left for Trinidad that first time?

It was this intense dichotomy you always feel in Jamaica, living in heaven and living in hell at the same time.

Jamaican alarm clock.

LJ: I think it was just a day or two.

RS: So you didn't really get the chance to get the feel of the place?

LJ: No.

RS: And you flew to Trinidad for Carnival. How long did you spend there total?

LJ: Just a couple of days, three, four days. You know, on the way we stopped at different islands, just 'cause we had this plane and we could stop. We stopped in Martinique. Martinique was nice. I know we stopped in Tobago. On the way back we stopped in Haiti. That was quite an experience.

RS: You know, people told me, when I spoke in Martinique in 1999, that Bob had been in Martinique, and I said, this doesn't sound right, I've never heard of this.

LJ: He absolutely was!

RS: Was he actually on the ground? Did you go to the market?

LJ: Yeah, we went to the beach and toured around a little. I don't remember if we stayed overnight or not. Martinique was beautiful, I remember the girls were so beautiful.

RS: It's still gorgeous, and Bob is God in Martinique, Bob is like the national hero. His picture is absolutely everywhere, he's on the air all the time.

LJ: Sorry we can't go there now. I'd like to go there with him. Yeah, we liked Martinique, people were smiling, as opposed to Haiti.

RS: Did you spend any time in Tobago?

LJ: No, we'd just go to the beach, have fun. I was like, this is the Traffic and Chris Blackwell world. This is how rock and roll royalty takes vacations. It was new to me, but don't get me wrong, I was thinking, this is easy to get used to. And yet, here I was with this revolutionary from the shantytowns and it was very confusing. I tried to formulate this idealized view of Chris as not really being the quintessential capitalist but really being a subversive. I was wrong, but i was also right.

RS: And then you went to Port of Spain probably?

LJ: Yeah, and Chris knew some people there. We stayed in somebody's house, very spiffy and kind of upper-class Caribbean; you know how it is—colonialist. Everyone light-skinned. And there were two beautiful sisters in their early twenties, Trinidadian. Their name was Gibbs, and it was their family's house. Some years later they were thrown out of the eleventh floor window of Chris's suite at the Windsor Hotel in New York, where I had first met Bob, by one of their boyfriends, who then got in the elevator, walked out of the hotel to the corner, down the stairs to the subway, put a token in the turnstile, and then jumped in front of the first passing train. He was a musician, had a band, was college educated, and was also from an upper-class Trinidadian family, and I often wondered what had gone on in that New York hotel suite, to so tragically craze this intelligent, talented young man.

Stopping on the roadside near Bluefields on the southwest coast to drink two jellies and chill with a nice draw. (left to right: Champs (so named for being Jamaica's top herb dealer), Sledger, Peter Tosh, LJ.)

30.

"out of many... one people"

LJ: Well, yeah, you know we moved uptown into 56 Hope Road, and it's right down the block from the Prime Minister—

RS: But we're jumping ahead. I set that up that way because I was wondering if there was any of that feeling among maybe the servants in the house where you were staying, if they kind of looked sideways at Bob when they saw him come in there in Trinidad?

LJ: He didn't have locks really then, they were just starting. He looked more like an American guy with an Afro or something.

RS: So did you go down immediately to Carnival when you arrived in Trinidad?

LJ: Yeah, Carnival was starting, that was it, Carnival was everywhere.

RS: Tell me about the experience. Did Bob dance in the street? Did anybody recognize him?

LJ: No, nobody recognized him, Bob was obscure. Outside of Trench Town, nobody knew him. In Jamaica, when you drove around with Bob, people on the street knew him, at least in the poor neighborhoods.

RS: Even early on when you were with him?

LJ: Oh, yeah! He was a hero in Trench Town, Ghost Town, all the hard-core ghetto places. And we'd go to the country and it seemed incredible how the country people knew him—like a son or a brother or a nephew and I could never tell, when people would offer us their best herbs or ital food [no salt, no meat] or just best wishes if they had nothing else to give—if they really knew him or were actually related, or just knew him because he was in the Wailers and loved him for the music and the joy and hope the music would always bring. And we'd stop at the tiny roadside shops of rusted tin and wood and they'd always have a jukebox and there'd always be a few classic old Wailers singles and I'd want to stop at every one of these shops because there might be a Wailers record I hadn't heard. And I can remember hearing "Trench Town Rock" for the first time at one of these places on a winding mountain road on a lazy golden late afternoon in St. Ann's Parish, on our way to Nine Mile where Bob was born, on which he sang, "Hit me with music, when it hits you feel no pain." No recording had ever moved me like that. I must have been shaking I was so blown away, and Bob had gone around to the back of the shop to look at some herb and roll a spliff and I just needed to hear that song over and over again, the scratchy vinyl 45 emanating from the ancient machine, and Bob came around the front of the store

and saw me and said, "Whappen to you, mon?" And I opened my mouth to try and say something but it just stayed open with nothing coming out and Bob joked, "Look like a duppy get you mon!"—meaning I looked like a ghost had possessed me—and finally I said, "That's the greatest record I ever heard." And he threw his arm around my shoulder and he just started to laugh, and then we were both laughing and he handed me his spliff, which he had just lit, and he said, "Take this spliff, Lee Jah-free, you need a good draw to scare dem duppy away."

R: But in Trinidad there was no reggae at all probably.

L: Nobody knew who Bob was, the same as middle-class, upper-class Jamaicans did not know who he was. He meant zero, nothing, nada.

RS: Even after ten years of his music career at that point?

LJ: He meant nothing, he was just another reggae singer. Wasn't any different than Toots and the Maytals or John Holt or any other reggae star, just an entertainer.

RS: They were just ghetto people.

LJ: Yeah, they were all the same.

RS: So he was anonymous in Trinidad.

LJ: We were totally anonymous.

RS: What was it like to be with Bob Marley at Carnival?

LJ: Bob couldn't find anything to smoke. We were out of smoke by the time we got there, and we could find nothing to smoke. And we wrote this song about how we didn't like Trinidad, we didn't like your Carnival, and there was nothing to smoke, and blah-blah-blah.

RS: Did he ever record it?

LJ: I don't think so, no.

RS: "Trinidad We Don't Like Your Carnival"—is that what it would have been called?

Lee Jaffe, NYC 1975

LJ: Yeah (laughs), something like that. Yeah, because this was after three days of nothing to smoke, and everybody's completely drunk.

RS: Even Bob?

LJ: No! We didn't drink, you know, so everybody else is drunk and jumping around

The house I helped build with Esther and Bob at Little Bay on the south coast between Negril and Savanna-La-Mar.

to this really fast music, and we're like—everybody's having this great time and we can't even get a spliff.

RS: So, was Bob dancing in the streets?

LJ: No!

RS: You were just watching?

LJ: Yeah, it was just like we were completely distant, from another world.

RS: Did you walk through the streets, did you just have one vantage point?

Winston Anderson with a bamboo pipe he invented to steam herb.

LJ: Yeah, we walked through the streets, we watched the thing, and it was kind of fun for the drummers, but after a day or so, we definitely weren't into it. It was definitely an alcohol world, and we were definitely not in that world. Everybody was drunk for three or four days. We were not into that. And we couldn't get anything to smoke, so this got really annoying after three days, you really wanted to leave.

RS: Would you go home every night to the house or did you stay out all night?

LJ: Well, you couldn't sleep, you know, because everybody's up. We were tired.

RS: So your nerves must have been on edge after a couple of days of this.

LJ: Yeah, we were really happy to leave.

RS: Anything else about that experience that you remember particularly?

LJ: I remember Haiti—we were returning to Jamaica and the last place [en route] is Haiti, and you can't just land. You have to give twenty-four-hour notice to land in Haiti, which we hadn't done, and we were going, "Oh, it's Haiti! Oh, let's go to Haiti!" So—

LJ: Yeah—oh, it's Haiti. Let's go to Haiti! That's the way we were doing it, we were stopping at all different islands. We had the pilot wiring "engine trouble." So, you know, we're on the road for ten days, after Carnival we looked like this band of revolutionaries. We touched down at the airport at Port-au-Prince and we get out of the plane and it's surrounded by two hundred Ton Ton Macoute with machine guns pointed at us. Now this is the situation: you're on an island, you're on Haiti. This is Papa Doc! And Baby Doc, one of them in power. And we got off the plane, and they put us in these vans and took us someplace. I didn't know where they were taking us, and it was scary. They put us in this hotel. I was thrilled it was a hotel. The hotel had a casino and we weren't allowed to leave. We were under house arrest. And I remember the casino was right out of Graham Greene, it was French, colonialist, but it was black, everyone was very, very black, there were like no light-skinned people. Everyone well-dressed—the croupier perfectly attired, and it felt like a time warp, as if it were the 1940s and there was a world war going on, but we were not part of the world.

RS: Panama hats and wide lapels and stuff? Sydney Greenstreet?

LJ: Yeah, it was definitely classic.

RS: Now Bob wasn't into gambling, so he didn't want to go down to the casino?

Madaline Scott, my girlfriend at her family's house, Blue Harbour in Port Maria on the north coast.

LJ: Not really, although he'd occasionally gone to the track. But he wasn't interested in the casino. And then I remember the next morning we were leaving, and somehow Esther and I left in one van, and Bob somehow thought he was getting

Esther Anderson with her brother Winston and his wife Princess. I am in the background. Negril, Jamaica 1973.

left behind. And it was really sad because his father, who was a white Jamaican born in Clarendon, had deserted him, and now he was being left on this island, where hundreds of very black Ton Ton Macoute in ill-fitting shark-skin suits and pork pie hats, never sweating though the sun was blistering, had greeted us with scores of very fascist-looking army-fatigued militia, all with machine guns pointed at our eyes, and had been escorting us around, making sure whatever thoughts of fomenting revolution on this most impoverished country of the Western hemisphere, where secret police kept the populace in a state of constant fear for the benefit of the tiny elite ruling class, would be squashed, aborted, and here we were, and if they could read our minds, so guilty and dead with just the slightest movement of a finger, however accidental. All the nuances and feelings of Jamaica's particularly flavored racism, surfacing, feeling red, so mulatto and condemned, neither black nor white, and his new movie star Jamaican lover with whom he felt so immediately and deeply connected, she being light-skinned and straight-haired, with whom he had hoped to learn so much about navigating in the white world, and his new revolutionary best friend, his first and maybe last white best friend, who understood the all-importance of the message of his music as they too, if only inadvertently, for just an instant, were deserting him. And it was sad because we had built up such a trust, and I knew that I was the first white person he ever trusted, and I could see and smell the fear like the coal fires that burnt everywhere in Port-au-Prince, and the commonplace terror on the people's faces, and I knew it was lost, that aura of innocence that had surrounded us, and I knew it would be always a struggle for us to enter that rarefied world again. And he came in another van and came separately, and he was pissed! He thought we were deserting him, he was so pissed! That was the first time I had seen Bob pissed off. It was scary, it was really, really scary. It was, "How could you leave me surrounded by fascists, deranged, speaking some foreign language?"

RS: So you had no experience of the island other than the hotel?

LJ: Right.

RS: You couldn't go out and walk the streets, you couldn't look for music?

LJ: No, no. They escorted us back to our plane after they had checked out the engine trouble and the plane was OK.

RS: So you were just there overnight.

LJ: Yeah.

RS: To the best of your knowledge did Bob ever go back to Haiti?

LJ: I would be shocked if he ever went to Haiti. He had been afraid that he thought we were leaving him behind. He was so pissed! (laughs) I mean, obviously we wouldn't leave him behind. But everyone on this trip was new to him. He hardly even knew Chris Blackwell. He had gone to England to finish *Catch A Fire*, so he'd spent a few weeks there. But Chris was new in his life too. And he didn't know any of the other people, and Esther Anderson, he had just met Esther and me. And he had just had this experience which I didn't know about at the time of being abandoned in Sweden with no money by Danny Sims, his former manager. So I think he was a little paranoid anyway.

Multiple exposure Polaroid, Negril, Jamaica 1973.

After Carnival in Trinidad: Early 1973

The wind hot and crimson circling clouds streaming lavenders and lapis darkening as a near full moon burning silver rose while the last scraps of daylight dipped and dissolved sinking down through Carribbean horizon in the lazying forlorn west. My harmonica wailed mournful blues from the back seat of Bob's Capri as Esther chatted nonstop from the shotgun side, Bob maneuvering around potholes—while listening intently—deftly and with a supreme concentration.

We weaved and stuttered our way through to Port Royal, where some three hundred years before a great earthquake had destroyed what was the most bustling town of the whole West Indies: where pirates Morgan and Cook and Bluebeard whored, where slave ships routinely dumped their human cargo, the worthwhile remains to be bartered and auctioned after the interminable voyages from West Africa, during which less than half would survive in the seasick starving galleys in chains and emerging half or three quarters dead from the ship's hull squinting, iron clanging in the searing white hot sun from their allotted positions arm to arm head to feet, not an inch wasted, calculated, diagrammed, packaged, the proprietors knowing more or less how many would perish in the premeditated mass murder of beasts of burden needed to cut the cane to be boiled into molasses from which would be extracted and bleached white and therefore pure—sugar—to sweet the fancy of the white-wigged pale and powdered white-faced lords and

Al Anderson, the day he first arrived in Jamaica.

ladies of the boundary-less queendom called the British Empire.

And what remains... A cannon, a fort ruined beyond ruins. A town of ghosts whistling faint discordant ballads and jigs cacophonic—fleeing in and out of consciousness, turning curtly, violently, to catch what was there or what is not.

We curled through a roundabout and out to the desolate dark harbor, where some dozen women with kerosene lamps sold various fried fish— snapper, jack, king, and sprat— from creaky wooden tables, topped by flimsy glass cabinets glowing faintly in the hazy firelight. I could imagine these women, some maga with craggy skin, some round and oversized with fatty bum-bums in their day jobs, pounding the cassava root with wooden mallets into quarter-inch thick cakes to be fried and sold with the fish—salted and therefore un-ital—the yellow-white chewy—called bammie.

And Esther ranting about how the Spanish and then the English came to obliterate the indigenous people, the Caribs and the Tainos, their Arawak language centuries-lost, and me in my stern silence acknowledging what I knew to be true, and Bob in turn sensing

Big Youth. Years before there was anything called "rap," he was one of the first people to become a star sole-
ly for his talent for talking on top of a rhythm track. In the early seventies he dominated the Jamaican music
charts, sometimes with three or four singles in the top ten simultaneously.

the white youth so recalcitrant, implaca-
ble in his revolutionary zeal.

   We chose the fish we wanted
from the various ladies wishing for a
sale and Esther begged me to take a
piece of bammie to go with them. They
served the poor man's feast in white
newsprint-like paper, and we mean-
dered out onto a dilapidated wooden
pier that extended some twenty yards
out into the near-still water. I could see
the tangerine lights of Kingston pulsing
across the bay, the sky argentous, scintillating—the breeze dreamy, warm,
wistful.

   "You know cassava was more than just a root to be mashed up and fried for the original
people here, Lee Jaffe," Esther continued as if in some remote way in my whiteness I too might
need to take on some responsibility for the iniquitous Iberian legacy.

   "It was a sacred t'ing for the Tainos. They believed in a superior being, a life-giving force
they called Yucahu, and Yucahu represented sea and cassava because both were never-failing
sources of sustenance. They sat here six hundred years ago and ate the same t'ing we a-nyam
now." She laughed. "A true, mon...

   "And the Spanish a wicked, you see, mon? Dem would string dem poor innocents up by
dem raas feet and light a fire beneet dem and laugh while dey watched dem slowly burn. Or dem
would play games by seeing who could chop up an Indian de fastest and then feed dem to some

vicious dogs they did a-bring wit' dem
from Spain. They made slaves of them to
dig in mines for gold, but dem never find
no raas gold a Jamaica, and some of
dem would run away or just hang dem-
selves, whole families, children too,
rather than subjugate themselves to de
pernicious blood-claat who did call themselves Christians."

   I suffered Esther's ravings which,
on the one hand, seemed directed at me,
and on the other were for Bob, to show
off her radical social consciousness, but I
couldn't help but smile, the fish being so
succulent, the bammie sweet from the

coconut oil. Then Bob produced three twelve-ounce bottles of a creamy white liquid and passed them around.

"What's this?" I asked of the label-less bottles.

"Irish moss and soursop juice," Bob replied with the assured confidence that this would blow my mind. "Ital, mon. No sugar, no condemned milk. Only honey use fe sweeten it." And yes, it was smooth and as dreamy as the soft wind lilting through the coconut trees. Then magically, as if scripted by Jah, some Christmas tree–like buds appeared. "Lamb's bread, mon. I and I get eet from Sledger who helped grow eet a St. Ann's, the parish dem call Jah's parish, the parish where I and I a born. Lamb's bread a special herb a hard for get eet, seen?"

"Can we go there? I want to see the country. I want to see where you come from."

"Yeah, mon. We can reach dem parts dere."

"And can we actually go to the herb field where this came from?" Bob laughed.

"You want to see every t'ing, Lee Jaffe..." Esther chimed in.

"Go for me guitar, my youth," said Bob, as he rolled separate huge cone-like spliffs for each of us.

I bounded to the car to get Bob's acoustic. I could sense the inchoate stirrings of word and music brewing in a soul born of disparate continents. In a soul wailing, tormented with the burden of the criminally poor, the indigent, the starving, and the destitute of the shanty towns from Kingston to Cape Town, from Bed-Stuy to the stilted slums of

Bunny Wailer playing football. A constant source of enjoyment, whether in the ghetto at Boys Town or on a dirt field on the outskirts of Kingston.

Bangkok. But a soul also so free in the mellow moonlight glistening off the tropical sea mingling with the lamp lights and the open wood fires, a soul uplifted by the gift of Jah's good herb and the intoxication of love at first sight with his Jamaican East Indian peasant-born entertaindom-royalty

Robbie Shakespeare and Al Anderson on the road during the Legalize It tour.

princess who through a simple phone call—"forget that Hollywood crap and go make a good movie"—had the power to resurrect the languishing career of her ex-boyfriend Marlon Brando and at the same time igniting the career of a budding Italian cineaste Bernardo Bertolucci, her call being the catalyst for what would become *Last Tango in Paris*. Bob took a long, slow draw off the extravagant spliff, the fire tip glowing amber as I passed him his guitar. Then lighting my own while taking in the celestial night sky more rich with glitter than any I'd to that moment witnessed, I began to follow the ethereal rhythm of his right hand against the steel strings with my trusty D harp, my breathing in and out caressing the metal reeds, careful to augment and not overwhelm his guitar, leaving space for his voice to be intimate without straining. And Bob began to sing:

So Jah say
not one of my seeds shall sit in the sidewalk and beg
your bread
(No they can't and you know that they won't)
So Jah say
you are the sheep of my pasture
so verily, thou shall be very well...
and down here in the ghetto
and down here we suffer
I & I a-hang on in there and I & I, naw leggo

for so Jah say…

So Jah seh, "Not one of my seeds shall sit in the sidewalk and beg bread."

— BOB MARLEY

Bob reading the Bible up the hill from the house where he was born at Nine Mile, St. Ann's Parish, Jamaica.

LJ: Winter 1973.

RS: Joe Higgs was living there too?

LJ: Yeah. Dickie Jobson had arranged for him to make a record with Eric Gale, the great r&b/jazz guitar player from Jamaica who had been living in the States for many years. And there's actually lots of beautiful things on there, but somehow the record never really got finished in the right way. But there's some beautiful stuff on there. In fact, I co-wrote the title song of Joe Higgs' album, which was finally released as *Life of Contradiction*. And I'm credited, but my name's misspelled, Jaffrey or Jeffree, Lee Jaffrey. And Esther contributed too.

RS: Did you write it at Hope Road?

LJ: Yeah.

RS: So at this point Blackwell had bought 56 Hope Road?

LJ: Bought 56 Hope Road, he was going to invest more in reggae now.

RS: Was Cindy Breakspeare [Bob's white Jamaican girlfriend and mother of Damian Marley, and the former "Miss World"] living in the house when you started living there?

LJ: She was working there.

RS: She had an apartment in that house for a while, in around '74–'75, she told me herself.

LJ: An apartment in the house?

RS: Or a room.

LJ: Don't remember. I thought she was living down the road. She was there every day. She and this other really beautiful girl, I think her name was Victoria, and they might have been doing things for Chris or Dickie Jobson.

RS: For the label, or other interests?

LJ: Whatever things had to be done.

48.

To me, this was the most amazing couple, they were awesome! When you saw them together, the visual thing of it was so intense. They were just so high, you just wanted to be around them they were just so compelling, you could not not look at them

RS: And was the old lady still in the house too, who originally owned it?

LJ: No, but I remember the caretaker, Rennie. He was like a holdover from slavery, in a colonial house, the back house is the slave quarters and Rennie lived in the back next to the slave quarters, and he was like the slave of the place. He never progressed an inch out of slavery consciousness, and unfortunately there were a multitude like him in Jamaica and he got paid maybe ten dollars a week.

RS: And a bed to sleep on—

LJ: Yeah. He was a very kind man.

RS: What were his duties?

LJ: He was the gatekeeper, he'd look after the place, whatever had to be done, clean up.

RS: And other than that, was it all three Wailers hanging there, living there?

LJ: No.

RS: Was there anyone actually living there, or were they just using it as an office and rehearsal space?

LJ: We turned the back slave quarters into a rehearsal studio, and it was just Bob and me and Esther—'cause Bob was basically with Esther—that were living there. And it was really this big deal because they were this incredibly gorgeous couple, ghetto singer and movie star. When you saw the two of them they just looked so different. Esther was at the height of her beauty. Her acting career was happening, she was the big black star, even though she was not black, she was Indian and white. She had straight hair.

RS: Was she wealthy?

LJ: No, her mother was poor, living in the country. Her father was an architect. I never met him. I think he was Scottish, and she was raised by her mom in the town of Esher in St. Mary, a little town up in the hills, totally country, very tiny remote town. And she had an incredible brother who was a dreadlocks, but of the purest kind of ital Rastaman where he's a total vegetarian, wouldn't eat anything dead—an astute, very brilliant philosophical person, who lived off farming. He made these pipes. He had developed a pipe where you don't really smoke

the herb, you steam it. Made out of bamboo, and some water goes in some place, and you just kind of sip on it, you don't really inhale it, and we'd get really high. It was to save your lungs. It had a metal cup that sat on top of the bowl that held the herb and you'd put some hot coals in it and the herb would just steam. It was a very beautiful way of smoking that he invented.

RS: And you introduced Esther to Bob?

LJ: Yeah, I was about to make a movie, I had just made a movie in France, a fifty minute film. It wasn't even finished yet, but I had had some screenings of the unfinished version. Henri Langois showed it at the Cinémathèque, and it was kind of very well received in the Paris underground film world. I had great people in it.

RS: What was the story?

LJ: It was the story of a French TV star whose public image was a very straight tie-and-jacket type of thing, very conservative. But in real life he was living in a rundown house in Clichy, a thirteen-room mansion which had become this commune, and he was doing heroin. A lot of people were doing heroin. And it was kind of the end of the hippie era, that's kind of what it's about. There was no script, everything was improvised. I was twenty years old at the time, an American in Paris. My assistant director was Marguerite Duras's son. And I had a brilliant young cinematographer, Bruno Nueyten, who went on to become highly regarded in France and then to direct the film *Camille Claudel,* starring Isabel Adjani, the mother of his child. So I had great people working. It was a beautiful-looking film, black and white, very, very, very grainy. We used high-speed film, pushed it past the maximum. We tried to make every element of the picture as radical as possible.

RS: Do you still have a copy?

LJ: No, but someone does in France. So before even finishing this film, I was off to make my next film. It was going to be about the search for this root that the Indians use in the Andes called che cha, a psychedelic root they use for mystical purposes. And again there was going to be no script, and I just tried to gather what seemed to me to be the most interesting young actors in France, people I felt might be able to embrace what I was trying to do. And somehow I was able to get Esther involved, through my girlfriend in France who was friends with her. And

Bob in Trench Town at the football field in the ghetto where we would go nearly every afternoon to play and "reason" and "lick a chalice"...

53.

Bob believed me when I told him his vast potential audience wanted to see him as he was in real life. With Al Anderson at the National Stadium, Kingston, Jamaica, 1974.

With Al Anderson and Family Man at the National Stadium, Kingston, Jamaica.

this was great, because she was such an extraordinary talent and exotic beauty. And then Esther helped me get Maria Schneider, who was finishing shooting *Last Tango in Paris*. I went to the set to talk to her. I had tea with Marlon Brando in a little café on the Seine just next to where they were shooting a scene on a bridge. We talked about [Gillo] Pontecorvo, and I told him with sincerity how much I admired the John Houston film he had done, which was his last picture, *Reflections in a Golden Eye*, which was such a commercial and critical failure. I talked to him about the film I was going to make in South America and he listened very intently. I'm thinking, I'm with Marlon Brando and he's talking to me about *The Battle of Algiers* and I'm talking about a bunch of freaks in the Andes trying to find some new way to get high. And I thought better than to ask him to be in my film, because I thought I should concentrate on getting Maria, who was still unknown, and not mess up my chances with her, and I had the precociousness to think, I'll do this film and it'll be radical and I'll get him for my next one. I really thought that. Then I talked to Maria about going to Chile and she was genuinely interested. I had a great cast. Besides Esther and Maria I had Jean-Pierre Kalfon, Pierre Clementi, who had just gotten out of prison in Italy for two years for possession of hashish, after having done Buñuel's *Belle du Jour*, and Zou Zou, who had just starred in Eric Rohmer's *Claire's Knee*. The plan was for everybody to come to New York and then go to Chile. I had someone in New York who was putting up some money, and I had somebody in Chile who was going to put up all the gear in Chile and make all of the arrangements. And Maria came: *Last Tango* was opening. It was the week in New York I met Bob.

RS: Now Bob didn't go to see *Last Tango in Paris*, did he?

LJ: Maybe. I don't really remember. He met Maria, though, because we were hanging out. Yeah, he must have come. It was a big opening, a gala thing, and Maria ended up on the cover of both *Time* and *Newsweek* the same week. It was like the first time that ever happened. They never do that to each other, it could only happen by accident. And it was a big comeback for Brando, because he had

Bunny and Bob. National Stadium, Kingston, Jamaica. Oct. 4th, 1975.

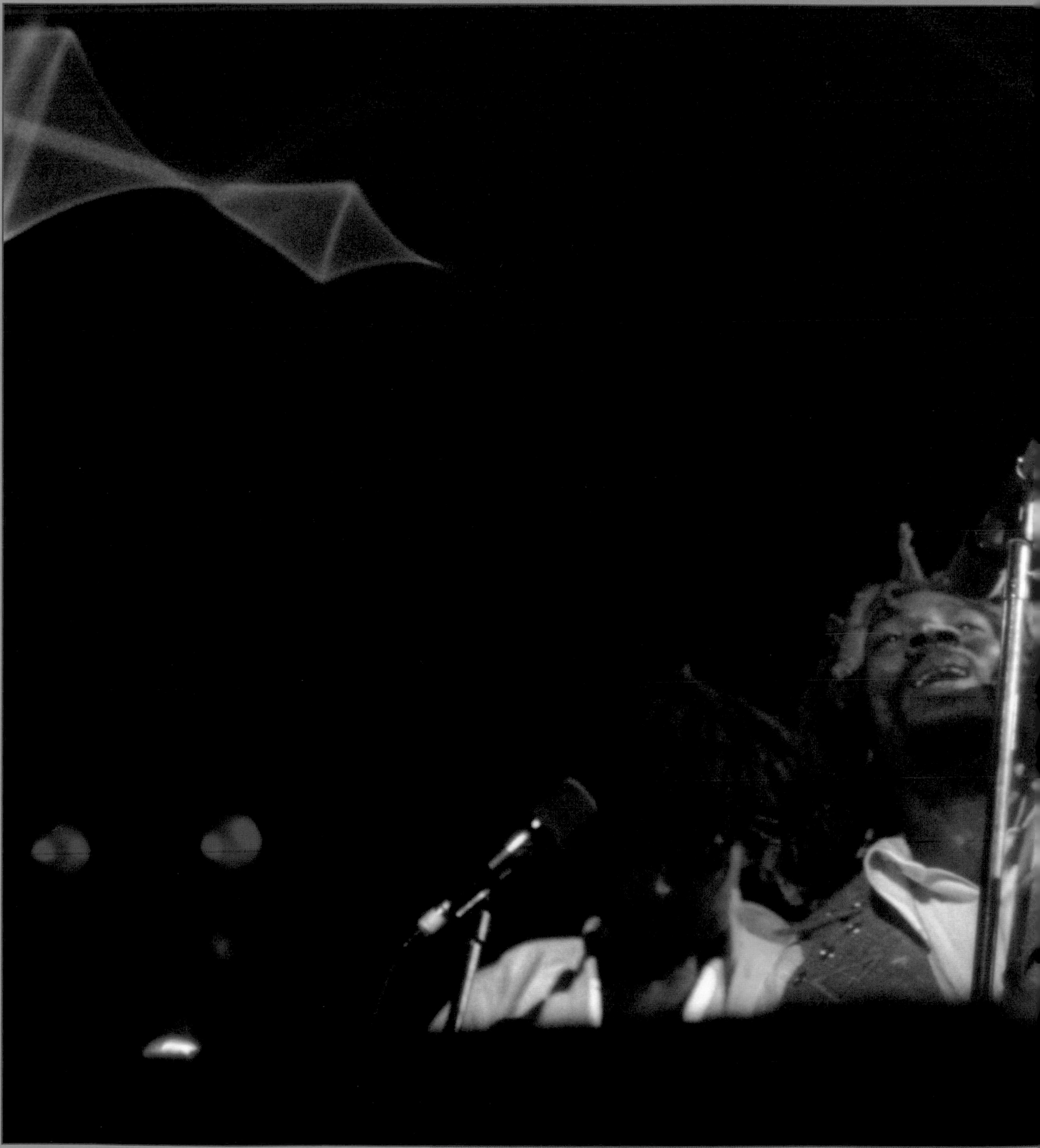

Peter, Bunny and Bob. Kingston, Jamaica, Oct. 4, 1975, on the same bill with Stevie Wonder. The last time the three original Wailers would perform together. I never witnessed any animosity between them and don't believe there was any—only tremendous respect.

just made all these flops and it'd been about five or six years since he made any movie that made any money. His career was at a low point, and yet it was considered a radical thing for him to go and make this movie with this foreign director.

RS: And this is the point at which you introduced Esther to Bob?

LJ: Right.

RS: Did sparks fly right away? What do you remember of that meeting?

LJ: Yeah, there was definitely an immediate infatuation. I mean, for Bob it was like why not? He's just like, wow, I'm with this movie star. But Esther, you know, was like, oh, Chris just signed this guy, right?

RS: Esther didn't know who he was, Esther didn't know his music?

LJ: Well, she knew that Chris had just signed this Jamaican group, the Wailers. It wasn't Bob Marley and the Wailers.

RS: But she's Jamaican. He's been making records for ten years in Jamaica.

LJ: Yeah, but Bob was not something special outside of the ghetto. Esther's living in England, and she was living in another world. She was an investor in Island Records.

RS: She's one of the founders.

LJ: Yeah, she already had her career when Island Records was starting. She had been living in England for five or six years or more. She was living with Mark

Carlton Barrett. His sense of humor, combined with a revolutionary zeal, created a dichotomy in his playing that was a perfect match for the lyrical content of the Wailers' songs.

Stevie Wonder jamming with the Wailers at National Stadium, Kingston, Jamaica. Later he would have a big American pop hit (something the Wailers never had) with the song "Master Blaster," inspired by the event.

64.

Peploe, who wrote all these Bertolucci movies, including *Last Emperor*. He also wrote *The Passenger* for Antonioni. So she was in a very different world than the one she was brought up in. Mark Peploe comes from a very upper-crust English family, very white aristocrats. That's the world she was living in. She wouldn't necessarily have known all the singles the Wailers had put out. But, of course, now that Chris had signed this group and, you know, Chris's whole aura was of someone of

great musical taste who was bringing r&b and blues to England and influencing musicians and all kinds of people, so Island signing a Jamaican band would certainly pique Esther's curiosity.

RS: And Esther's a country girl, and Bob's a country boy from Nine Mile, so they had—

LJ: They had a very visceral connection, they came from the same place, just down

Bob with guitarist Al Anderson and bassist Aston "Family Man" Barrett. Bob loved his Gibson SG. It was lightweight and easy to move with. The natural wood finish fit with the whole earthy Rastaman feel—the jeans, the dreadlocks. I told Bob to go onstage as you are in real life—make no distinction, no compromise—your audience will love you for it. Family Man—solid, unrelenting—the foundation of the music.

Peter Tosh, Bunny Wailer and Bob Marley; Kingston, Jamaica, Oct. 4, 1975.

the road basically in the next parish. Their roots were in the same rich deep red earth.

RS: So were you amused to see this develop so quickly?

LJ: To me, this was the most amazing couple, they were awesome! When you saw them together, the visual thing of it was so intense. They were just so high, you just wanted to be around them they were just so compelling, you could not not look at them. And their personalities were so intense. You know, Esther never stopped talking. And Esther too, in

some kind of way, it was chic to be politically radical, especially in the circles that Esther was rolling in. Because obviously she was always the outsider, right, so she had to be the voice of the people too. So here was this guy, the poet from the ghetto, it was just a natural thing for her to be with him. It was intense, it was immediate, it was Esther falling in love. Esther's thing with Mark Peploe was ending anyway. It wasn't like she met Bob and left Mark Peploe. They had already broken up, but they were still really good friends. And in fact, when I went to England, I would stay with Clare and Chloe Peploe, his sisters, and Clare eventually married Bertolucci.

house, while they were living in it—I guess with some publishing money from Johnny Nash, who had covered several of Bob's songs—out at Bull Bay, and she was physically constructing the house. She'd be carrying bags of cement and yet she was always radiant, glowing with a calm elegance regardless of what tenseness or chaos might be surrounding, she was and is extremely beautiful.

RS: Pregnant woman, carrying bags of cement—

LJ: She was incredible. And she'd be downtown every day running the Tuff Gong record store. They had this tiny little record store on Beeston Street. And this is downtown Kingston, it's hot there!

RS: In every sense.

LJ: Yeah, it's 108 degrees in the shade, and this is downtown Kingston, a tiny little storefront. And she ran it, and they sold their own records, and she would go to the pressing plant and have the records pressed, and see about the labels, and she was bringing up all these kids. And she had her own singing group, her own recording career, and she still had time to see that I had clean clothes. She was awesome.

RS: But she knew of Bob's relationship with Esther. She couldn't not know.

LJ: Well, recently Esther told me that Bob had always told her that Esther was with me. But you know it's Jamaica. Jamaican guys are supposed to have more than one

woman. It's a normal thing. If you don't, then something's wrong with you.

RS: Did you ever hear them argue about other women?

LJ: Occasionally they'd argue, but I never paid attention to what it was about. I had every reason for Rita and since Rita it was my place to be involved. One time, Bob and Rita raged at her, he reacted physically, to Jo-anne, her, and Rita told me that he threw something very pregnant – she told me.

RS: What was it about?

LJ: I don't know, really. I felt he was trying to make a point, and he knew Skill and I would stop him before anything serious would happen. There was so much pressure at the time, money pressure. I felt useless, like I should be helping more.

RS: You don't remember what triggered it?

LJ: No, no.

RS: Skill was also kind of Bob's manager and running Tuff Gong. He was even given a piece of Tuff Gong, he was the fourth partner at that point when you were there. This is according to Danny, Bob had set Skill up.

LJ: Yeah, well, you know Bob would do anything for Skill pretty much.

RS: Tell me about that relationship.

LJ: Well, Skill was a very likeable guy. Where is Skill?

RS: He married a woman last year in Detroit, so I don't know if he's living in Detroit. He was living in New Jersey.

LJ: Skill was a combination street hustler and prophet. He had a lot of the Bible memorized and could quote Scripture in any conversation. He also knew all the jockeys at the track. I remember once we got to the track early before the first race, it was Bob, Skill and Seeco, the Wailers' percussionist and myself– we were in the first row of the stands with very few people having arrived yet and the jockeys exercising the horses, when one came by us on a gray filly and to my amazement said out of the corner of his mouth, without breaking stride, "Sea Breeze in the seventh." Skill was a tremendous athlete. He was

Bob at Little Bay making ital food. >

a legendary soccer, football player. He had played in Brazil. When he came back from Brazil he had become a national hero. And he's also a kind of larger-than-life type character.

RS: How did Bunny and Peter feel about Skill?

LJ: Certainly he was a charismatic character and they had a lot of respect for him being such a great athlete. But I don't think they really understood why Bob trusted him as a business adviser. As far as their business, they didn't have the relationship that Bob had with him.

RS: During the first two years that you were in Jamaica, '73–'74, was Esther basically Bob's principal romantic interest?

LJ: Yeah. But she was more than that, although Bob did have some other affairs while he was on the road.

RS: When did their relationship end?

LJ: I think it kind of stopped around the end of '74, when Esther got sick and she had this operation and she couldn't have kids. I think Esther really wanted to have a kid with Bob, and it was just a big disappointment, and it just ended sadly.

RS: Lot of sadness at that time, with Yvonne [Peter Tosh's girlfriend] and everything else. [Yvonne died at the age of nineteen, having been in a coma for six months after a head-on collision between Peter's car and another, just outside of Kingston.]

LJ: Yeah, a lot of sadness. Incredible pressure.

RS: Great critical acclaim and no money.

LJ: No money, yeah.

RS: So you come back from Trinidad and you start living at Hope Road?

LJ: Yeah. It was a big house. I had one of the upstairs rooms. It was in the back. I think Bob and Esther had a room in the front part. I was in the back corner.

RS: Now you're a white guy in a very black environment, a very militant black environment with people like Peter Tosh around. How did people react to you?

LJ: Well, first of all, we were living uptown, so I blended more.

RS: Well, with the environment, but I'm talking specifically about 56 Hope Road, which was not full of white people.

LJ: No, but there were white people there. It was still Chris Blackwell's place and he had Cindy and this other girl, Diane Jobson, and Dickie Jobson, they're mostly white. So I became friends with Sally and Perry Henzell, that's an uptown white world. But then, of course, every day I'd go downtown with Bob. We'd make the rounds to Beeston Street, and we'd go to Trench Town every day.

RS: So who were the people Bob would check for in Trench Town on a given day of your rounds?

LJ: Well, Sledger was with us all the time, and driving a lot for us, Bob's cousin.

RS: He's a Malcolm?

LJ: He comes from Nine Mile, he must be a Malcolm.

RS: What was he like?

Ziggy Marley outside the Marley house near Bull Bay.

LJ: I loved Sledger. He was extremely kind, sensitive, at the same time he was a really tough guy. I always felt safe and protected when I was with Sledger. He was tall, lanky, with bright, attentive eyes. I felt he could sense danger before it became immediate and knew how to ward it off. He understood Bob's psyche really well.

RS: There were also some heavy cats around like Frowzer and Take Life, they were hanging out there too, weren't they, at Tuff Gong?

LJ: Yeah. They were bad youths from the ghetto that Bob said he was trying to reform. And we were making a lot of trips. Sledger, Esther, Bob, and myself, everwhere. The whole island. We would just drive all the time. It was the intractable, interminable search for the ultimate herb.

Rita Marley. Wife of Bob Marley, mother, singer, record company executive, her energy was interminable. Four young kids, pregnant, she was building a house near Bull Bay with her own hands while running the Tuff Gong record shop in downtown Kingston. Somehow she made sure I had clean clothes, and when I was arrested for herb and incarcerated for a week in Kingston Central, she made sure i had ital food to eat every day.

RS: In whose car?

LJ: In Bob's car, a European version of a Ford Capri. Sledger would drive, and sometimes Bob would drive, and sometimes I would drive. They kind of taught me how to drive in Jamaica. Left side of the road, but also how to avoid crucial things, to avoid potholes. You have to be tremendously artful. Because the cars, if you start hitting the potholes, these cars aren't going to last. Fixing it doesn't work, you can't get parts. So it becomes crucial not to hit the potholes. All the roads have potholes all over them. So you have to be incredibly in tune with not just what's around you but what's right underneath you, what's right in front on the ground. Knowing when to slow up for the potholes, so you can go around them, and avoiding children and animals. There would be children darting across the road at night or dusk and goats meandering seemingly oblivious. And we're driving all

The Wailers with the Jackson Five at 56 Hope Road.

Family Man, Bob, Bunny and unknown onlookers with Mrs. Jackson, the

hours, we're going all the time. Jamaica is 150 miles long by 50 miles wide, but there's 7,000-foot mountains that run right through the middle of it, and those roads are all dirt roads, so you can spend a lifetime literally driving around Jamaica and not find all of Jamaica. And Jamaica has amazing things in the interior. You're always coming across some amazing kind of landscapes, and tremendous fauna and flowers and fruits, always finding some new fruit, a new kind of banana. It's like seventy different kinds of mangoes, and they all have different names, and they all taste different, and have different texture and then you have to have a Bombay. And you get to know where there's a Bombay tree, and who might be having one on which side of which road. You'll drive an hour out of your way to get two ripe Bombays. That was my life.

RS: What kind of a driver was Bob?

LJ: Bob was an incredibly safe driver. I felt totally confident driving with Bob. I mean, he would drive fast, but he knew when to slow up. He was never out of control, I always felt that he had a tremendous aware-ness of trucks going by. If you were going around a curve, he would instinctively know that there was some out-of-control driver coming around. Somehow he knew, and he would be way off on the side of the road, and this guy would come down the middle of the road and if you were just dri-ving normally, you would have had a head-on collision. Sometimes it seemed he was clair-voyant behind the wheel.

Keyboard player "Touter" Harvey, Trench Town, 1973.

RS: So unlike driving with Peter you never felt unsafe with Bob?

LJ: That's correct.

RS: And driving with Peter was a very different experience.

LJ: Yes.

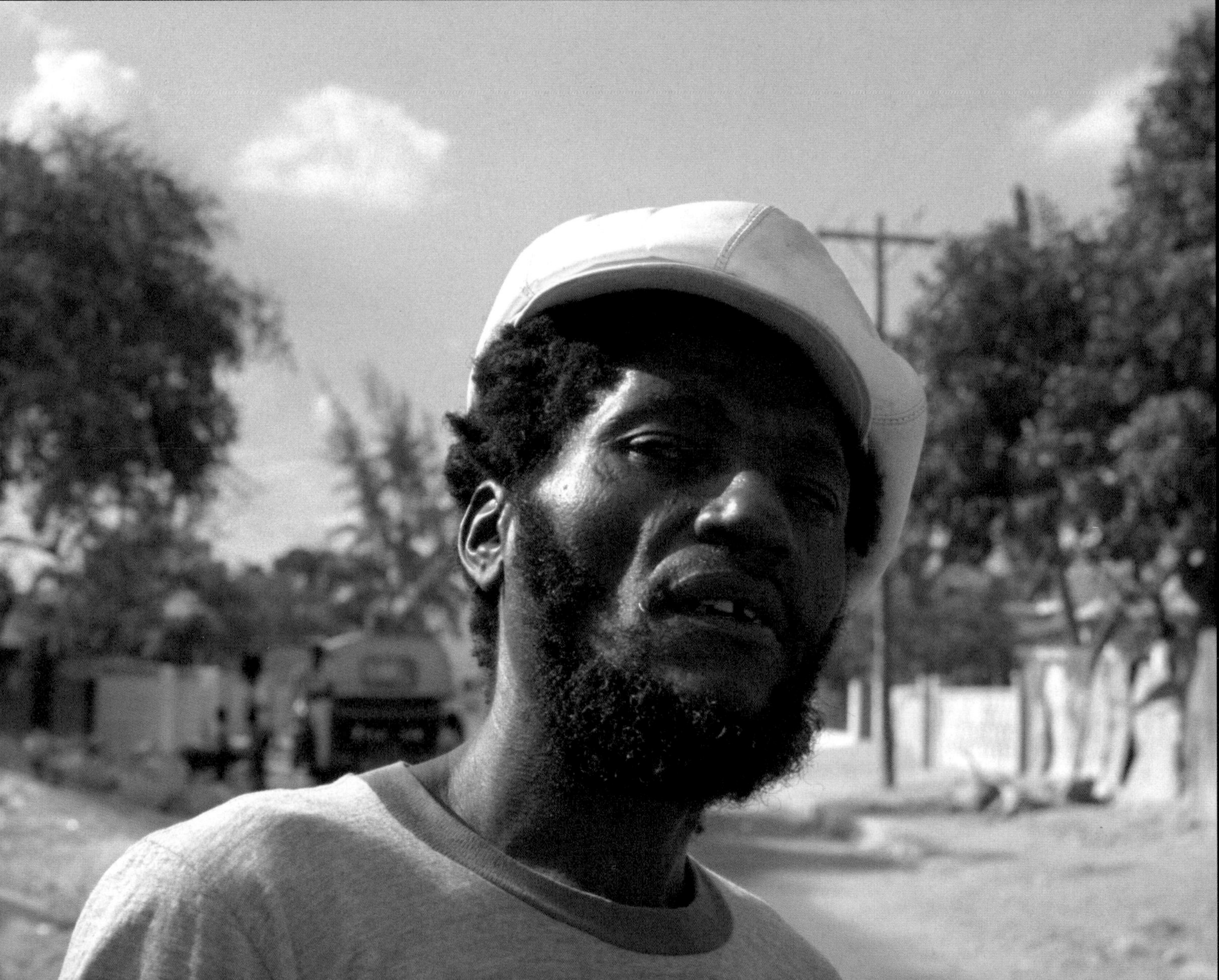

Tyrone Downey, keyboard player for the Wailers who eventually grew sick and tired of music after the tours ended and didn't entertain playing at notes at a freshman club through to the later years.

Joe Higgs in Los Angeles where he lived the last twenty years of his life and did much of the recording for his albums Blackman Know Yourself *and* Family.

RS: You really didn't want to be in a car with Peter driving.

LJ: That's correct.

RS: Why? Was he just not attentive, or he didn't have the skills of a good driver?

LJ: Peter was a totally reckless driver, he drove way out of control, drove way too fast in situations where he shouldn't have been driving that fast. And you knew that if anybody

came around a corner who didn't know what they were doing, he would not be able to save himself. And that's what happened. The same with Jacob Miller, the great lead singer of Inner Circle, who died behind the wheel. I wouldn't drive with him either.

RS: Tell me about the bust, or road block, that led to "Rebel Music (3 O'Clock Road Block)."

LJ: Well, that was when we were coming back from one of our many trips to Negril in 1974.

RS: At night?

LJ: At night.

RS: Who was in the car?

LJ: Esther, Bob and Sledger. And Esther had bought this property at my urging on the south coast about five miles from Negril.

RS: Is that where Bob built the cottage for her?

LJ: Well, we built this place together.

RS: Big high-pitched roof?

Carlton "Carly" Barrett, San Francisco, 1973, the Wailers' drummer and brother of Family Man.
Strong-willed, with a glowing, generous heart. Tragically Carly, like Peter Tosh, was to die by the gun.

LJ: Yeah. I have some pictures of it.

RS: So you actually helped physically build the place?

LJ: Yeah.

RS: And Bob too?

LJ: Yeah. You know, we had some people working on it but, yeah, that's correct. And we lived in it as the house was being built. So I had urged Esther to buy this land. It was just a few acres, and we kind of discovered it together, and she said, "Oh, I'll give you a half an acre for being here." I didn't have any money. And Esther bought it and I don't know if I own a half an acre there or not. (laughs) I guess not. And we used to go back and forth from there all the time, constantly.

RS: Were there any songs written there that you can remember specifically?

LJ: Bob was writing—well, "3 O'Clock Road Block" was written coming from there. It was at a time when there were a lot of

Aston "Family Man" Barrett at Cane River Falls.

road blocks and you always had to be careful. And I don't remember if it was before or after that I got caught in a road block and I was arrested, but—I think it was after—but we were driving, it was like three o'clock in the morning, and we just started singing that song, three o'clock road block. And I had my harmonica, I was always playing, and I think Sledger was driving, and I was just playing harmonica and Bob just came out with "three o'clock road block." And we just wrote the song right in the car.

RS: On the way back to Kingston?

LJ: Yeah, and then Bob gave writer credit to people who were not even there.

RS: Sure, that was on *Natty Dread*.

Aston "Family Man" Barrett. Fams, along with his brother, Carlton Barrett, comprised a rhythm section called the Upsetters and became the house rhythm section for producer Lee "Scratch" Perry and subsequently for the Wailers. Fams was a great teacher and helped bring many musicians forward with his tutelage. Bernard "Touter" Harvey, Tyrone Downey, Earl "Wya" Lindo, Robbie Shakespeare (who credits Fams for helping him as a teenager to transform his life from ghetto gunman to international star), and I were among his students.

LJ: Yeah. And then I was fortunate enough to play harmonica on the original recording. I remember Bob in the control room at Harry J's studio and I having trouble finding where to come in. I was so nervous and then Family Man finally came and stood next to me, and said, "When I tap you once"— and he tapped me on the shoulder—"you come in. When I tap you twice, you come out." And the control room was filled with people as it often was—Wailers and other musicians and hangers-on and Take Life and Frowzer, and having a harmonica was a novelty in reggae, and Bob had a spliff like some producer tycoon and he was beaming like he just became the biggest record company in the world and people in the control were pointing at me and nodding and cracking up laughing and I guessed it was okay or Bob would have stopped me. And then I knew it was all right cause I turned to Family Man and he said, "That's really good mon, let's go listen." And I'm thinking I never played on a record before and I'm going to be on an album with arguably the greatest band in existence.

RS: What else on that album did you have pieces of, in the creation of?

LJ: Well, that very directly. But most of the album came from Bob, just him and me playing. I don't know if I deserve writer's credits on any of the other songs, they really weren't mine. I was just blessed enough to be jamming with him when these incredible lyrics and melodies poured out of him. Bob was considered in the Rasta world to be like King David. And it all seemed very divine.

RS: You didn't throw any lines in here and there?

Tyrone Downey at his mother's yard, Kingston, Jamaica, 1975.

88.

LJ: No, it was really his lines and I was afraid to throw in lines by that point, because I had written "I Shot the Sheriff" with him and didn't get credit, and he certainly didn't need help with lines. I felt that if I threw in any lines and later didn't get credit, it would create bad feelings and I was just thrilled to be jamming with him and to witness these songs being created.

RS: Tell me the story about "I Shot the Sheriff."

LJ: That happened soon after we returned from Trinidad and we used to go out to a beach called Helshire.

RS: That's where Countryman lived.

LJ: Right. Countryman was one of the first people I met, because Dickie Jobson was friendly with Countryman, and whatever kind of luminaries would come to Jamaica via Chris or whatever, Dicko would be kind of a tour guide. And one of the first places he would take you would be to the beach—everybody wants to go to the beach. He would take you to Helshire, because Countryman was such a jovial, friendly kind of

guy, and he was sort of semi-Rasta, so much as he was becoming a dreadlocks and kind of looked like a Rasta, but at the same time he would cook you some lobsters. And shellfish, being scavengers, were something Rastas didn't eat. So he wasn't that much of a Rasta.

RS: Would Bob eat any of it?

LJ: No, no! No, definitely not. He didn't think of Countryman as a Rasta, 'cause Rastas don't eat that.

RS: Were he and Bob friendly?

LJ: Yeah, it was easy to be friendly with Countryman. We'd go out there, Esther, Bob, and myself, 'cause it was a beach close to town. The other beach I'd go to was Bull Bay. I'd go there most mornings at sunrise with Bob and Skill and run on the beach and up the hill to Cane River Falls. This was the beach where Bunny lived in a Rasta community.

RS: So Helshire was where "Sheriff" was born.

LJ: Yeah, it came out of me playing harmonica and Bob was playing guitar and Bob said, "I shot the sheriff" and I said, "But you didn't get the deputy." And that's how the song happened.

RS: What did you mean by that?

LJ: Well, it was a joke, you know, because they don't have sheriffs in Jamaica. Bob had a great sense of irony, he was a ready wit, so, you know, it was "I shot the sheriff," it was about him hanging out with this white guy, me. So it was like a comment about that.

RS: Were you the sheriff?

LJ: No, I wasn't the sheriff, but he was making—

RS: Did it come out of Western movies?

Tyrone Downey.

LJ: Yeah, it came out of Western movies, and here he was hanging out with this white guy, and it was said we were in a Western movie. You know, Jamaicans love Westerns. I think *The Good, the Bad and the Ugly* is always playing in Kingston. It seemed as if they were always rereleasing it—at that time you'd always see *The Good, the Bad and the Ugly* someplace.

RS: And it's a scene in *The Harder They Come*, "Hero can't dead till the last reel."

LJ: Right, right, right. So they're into that whole attitude, and here Bob was hanging out with this white guy, so it was like being in some Western movie with me.

RS: Did the song come fully sprung that day?

LJ: Yeah. According to Esther, she changed some stuff in England. And Bob changed some of my lines. I had a line— "all around in Kingston, the jeeps go round and round."

RS: What about "Freedom came my way one day"?

LJ: Yeah, that came after. That was written in England. Esther says that's her line.

RS: Was it ever called "I Shot the Police"?

LJ: Never!

RS: I've seen that in print.

LJ: (laughs) No, man, no. It came from Bob saying, "I shot the sheriff." And then I said, "But you didn't get the deputy." 'Cause he was making this joke, so I—and it was in falsetto. (Sings in high register, "I shot the sheriff.") But then the other part was supposed to be the bass line. (Sings low, "But you didn't get the deputy.") I wasn't there when they recorded it, when they did the vocals in England. They didn't send me to England, 'cause by that time I was not getting along with the Island Records establishment. Bob would have needed me in America, but in England he had Dicko, and I didn't really know England, so there was no

Bob at 56 Hope Road. A room on the upper floor facing north toward Mona and Papine and the Blue Mountains beyond. A place to light a spliff and laugh and reason. An uptown address just up the road from the Prime Minister's house, and although we weren't making much money and the house didn't belong to him yet, being there somehow felt like reaching the next plateau. Chris Blackwell bought this house with the idea that The Wailers (wailing over the sufferation in the ghetto) would take it over and "the dreads" certainly did. It was like saying here are "the dreads – the dreadful to look at"– your voices will resound every-where. Bob and Chris felt the significance of this and Bob loved Chris for making it happen.

reason to have me. And the expense of taking me to England was hard to justify because the band wasn't making any money.

RS: How were you able to really survive all this period?

LJ: I survived the same way everybody survived in the house on Hope Road.

RS: So if anybody had something, everybody had something, everybody ate. It was communal living, wasn't it?

LJ: I was with Bob all the time. He made sure that I ate.

RS: What did you do for pocket money?

LJ: I didn't have pocket money. I lived without money.

RS: So you really know how sufferers lived.

LJ: Yeah. It's like a line from a Dylan song, "When you ain't got nothin', you ain't got nothin' to lose." And I just went with it. I just looked at my life at that time as being presented with an opportunity that no one outside of Jamaica could possibly experience. The opportunity, also, through our music, to reach millions of people on a global scale and to have a powerful impact culturally, to raise people's consciousness, was everything I could have hoped for. I really had a utopian vision of this music really changing people's lives. But don't get me wrong, I was never hungry. I was eating the best food I had ever eaten. My diet completely changed. When I went to Jamaica I was like twenty-one, twenty-two years old, and I was moving at an accelerated pace. I was away from home and at college when I was sixteen and by the time I reached Jamaica I had already lived in Brazil for a year visiting the favellas with the great conceptual artist Helio Oiticica, making films with Rogerio Scanzala, Nevelle D'Almeida, and Miguel Rio Bronco, and jamming with Macale and Gal Costa. I had my

"Dirty Harry," the popular and jovial session player, who had a dry, sardonic wit. He recorded and toured with the Wailers. Later he was shot and killed in Brooklyn, New York.

work shown in a landmark show of conceptual art at the Museum of Modern Art in New York and was the youngest artist in the Paris Bienniel in 1970. I was convinced I wasn't going to live past thirty and I was determined to cram as much life into the next seven or eight years as possible. I had certain goals, and one of them was to be Muddy Waters's harmonica player. So when I met Bob and I kind of dropped everything to be in that world, it was like, okay, well maybe I'm not Muddy Waters's harp player, but I'm in the Wailers, and that might be just as good.

Al Anderson, lead guitar player for the Wailers on the Natty Dread album. He was from Montclair, New Jersey, and was just twenty-one years old when he met Bob in London in 1974. He had been living there for about a year and had become a popular session player at Island Studios when Chris Blackwell suggested he do overdubs on Natty Dread. Bob liked his playing and invited him to Jamaica. Being the only American among us I took it upon myself to help orient him to his new life. He had impeccable taste, and his deft and subtle leads on tracks like "No Woman No Cry," "Lively Up Yourself" and "Rebel Music (3 O'Clock Road Block)" helped to make these songs classics and to make the Natty Dread album more accessible to an American audience than previous Wailers albums had been. On the terrace of my West Side New York brownstone apartment around the time of the release of Legalize It, 1976.

RS: Were you ever on stage playing harmonica with the Wailers, anywhere?

LJ: Yeah, lots of places. Dozens of shows and up until now, along with the openings of my one-person shows at Moderna Museet in Stockholm and the Irish Museum of Modern Art in Dublin, those experiences rank as the most exciting work experiences of my life, and they are memories I will always cherish.

RS: Okay. Right after you came to Jamaica from Trinidad you must have met Bunny and Peter.

LJ: We didn't talk about "I Shot the Sheriff."

RS: Oh, oh, there's more to that?

LJ: Yeah. So we were just jamming, and then I remember there were these two really really fat girls dancing when Bob came out with that line. And then, it was like such a funny song, the beach wasn't that crowded, but we had a whole bunch of people just dancing to that song. I remember these two huge fat girls just dancing, and all these other people dancing around them. And Bob was playing guitar and I'm on harmonica. Then I wrote down all the lyrics that Bob was singing. And I was excited 'cause I knew it was a big song and I felt I was integral in its conception, and then I came up with the line "all along in Trench Town, the jeeps go round and round," 'cause the police and military drove jeeps and I was thinking of the curfews that were being called in the ghetto and what it was like for the poor people, the "sufferers," to live in a militarized zone and to have the basic freedom of walking in the street taken away and how it related to politics and the U.S. involvement in Southeast Asia and the C.I.A. pressure on the Caribbean and Latin America and I flashed on being on the beach in Rio in Ipanema, being with a girlfriend who was a radical student leader and she, pointing out a blonde, crewcut guy with his wife and two pre-teenage daughters relaxing on a Sunday morning and hipping me to the fact that he was an American sent by Nixon to train torturers, and I was thinking of what was taking place in Chile, and how the events there had resulted in my being in Jamaica, and what a genius Bob was for coming out with the line "I shot the sheriff" because, though it was funny, it was also so poignant, so relevant to the global repression, and later he changed the line to "All along in my home town" and that was better, because it made the point that these violent interventions into everyday life in the shanty towns of Jamaica were intrinsically foreign- influenced. And when I said, "But you didn't get the deputy," it was ironic and slighty self-deprecating, because what it was saying was, yeah, I got the balls to shoot the sheriff, but I don't have it together by myself to get all his backup. And this is going to be a long, tragic struggle that's going to need a lot of everyday heroes.

Blowing harmonica with The Wailers, Central Park, New York City, summer 1975. The Natty Dread tour. The backdrop for the stage was done by Nevil Garrick who went on to do all subsequent staging for the band as well as all album covers. His powerful and elegant work helped to visually define the Wailers. Photograph by Anton Mikofsky.

" LEGALIZE IT...
AND I WILL
ADVERTISE
IT... "

— PETER TOSH

Peter in his element. >

LJ: Yeah, so we're at Hope Road and it's this constant stream of people around Bob. So I just started to meet each person, from Joe Higgs to Family Man to Carly. And each person was more amazing than the next. Because I was only expecting to make this trip and stay for a little while, and then I didn't know what I was going to do about my movie. I just didn't know. And I mentioned earlier that the producer in Chile became "disappeared." That's how come I went to Jamaica. If that hadn't happened, I might never have seen Bob again.

RS: This is at the time of the coup that overthrew Allende in Chile?

LJ: Yeah. So I had this whole cast and crew come from France, and Esther from England. Maria Schneider was scheduled to do, I think, *The Passenger* next with Antonioni, but she had a window of opportunity before it was to start, so she agreed to be part of our adventure. And then we couldn't find our Chilean co-producer. I was feeling a lot of pressure, 'cause I had all these people that had traveled really far to converge in New York to make this trek to the Andes and I was feeling so helpless with that Chilean partner being missing, "disappeared," and the term "disappeared" was one that was new and ominous. So when the invitation to go to Jamaica came up, I took it in order to get away from all the stress I was feeling with everyone, all the talented people I had assembled just waiting around not knowing what would happen. And of course all these French people with too much time on their hands began to bicker about the movie. I had a very highly regarded young cinematographer named Michel Fournier, who people were saying was the big influence on Vittorio Storraro, who was working with Bertolucci. When we returned to Jamaica from our trip to Trinidad and it looked like through Esther's friend Perry Henzell, who had directed *The Harder They Come*, I could get all the equipment and support to shoot a film, I phoned to New York and spoke to Michel about the possibility of everyone just coming to Jamaica and we'd make something different, although I didn't know what. He simply told me, "I cannot shoot in Jamaica. Jamaica is too green." And that's the moment I knew that that movie was not meant to be. So I was at Hope Road now and it was just this constant stream of amazing people. And it seemed that whatever I had been doing paled compared to what they were into because not only were these people so amazingly talented, but what they were doing was so revolutionary and it fit into my whole political consciousness. If they were going to let me be here and contribute to this, whatever it was that I could possibly be doing someplace else could not be as important. So meeting Family and Carly and Joe Higgs and of course Peter and Bunny was awesome. They were articulate, powerful, focused on where they wanted to go and the message that they had and how to get it

out there, and were so incredibly uncompromising, that I was left defenseless. I couldn't think that any other mission could be more important. I knew that they were not going to compromise to get a hit record. It was the most fierce, pure attitude I had ever been confronted with, and it left me very humble. I had always considered my work radical, and to meet the Wailers and sense the enormity of what they were doing—well, I just wanted to be part of that. I knew absolutely it was where I wanted to be.

Of course Rasta believes in eternal life, in a living God, in a radical and spiritual environmentalism that presupposes that the earth is God's gift to all beings, and Rasta has a respect for the human body as the temple of the Lord. They look to Genesis, where it says that the food of man shall be fruits and herbs. And they embrace a vision of a self-sufficient agrarian society that could exist without the scourge of tourism, which raped the land of its natural beauty by constructing hotels of mindless architecture and perpetuated a colonial slave mentality among the workers needed to maintain its creeping cancerous sprawl. And I think of our innocence, the times we'd drive through the tropical countryside to the far western tip of the island to an hallucinatory paradise called Negril, with its seven-mile-long beach of peachy white sand leading to the magnificent coral cliffs and incandescent waters, where there were no phone lines yet and no electricity and only seven bamboo and mahoo houses with cedar floors and thatched roofs, and we were naive enough to think that maybe this far end of the island could become inhabited with a loving, nurturing attitude toward its natural beauty.

As much as I thought of myself as the romantic tragic revolutionary, there was also a bit of the cynic in me who believed in death and that I would not live past thirty. And now I was confronted with a culture that defied the existence of death, as in Peter Tosh's song "Burial," "no one's funeral, knotty nah go." And a transformation began to occur in me which turned me from an infatuation with death toward a love of life and acceptance of and humble gratitude for Jah's gift and the realization that whatever talent had been bestowed upon me was to be used to raise people's consciousness to help create a harmony and better overstanding among all peoples.

RS: You've said, and other people I know who were around at that time have said, that talking to any one of the Wailers was like talking to the other two, that they even sounded alike, that they were like one person, they were so close in all the important ways.

LJ: If they were in agreement, if that's what you mean.

RS: But more than just agreement, it was like a trinity coming from the same source.

LJ: Yeah.

RS: They were that tight.

Peter Tosh. The Bush Doctor majestic in the fields of frosty herb. >

The rich red earth of Westmoreland produces some of the island's best sensi.

"Legalize it and I will advertise it."

LJ: They were really, really tight. Spiritually and politically. I felt it in their music. They were amazing together. I guess it's a sad thing that they never got back together again to make another record.

RS: And I think it hurt all three of them that that didn't happen, because they all wanted to.

LJ: Yeah.

RS: What was Peter like when you first met him, first impressions?

LJ: Peter was very magnificent looking. He was a tremendously powerful presence, perfect features, must have been about 6'4", 6'5". Everything about him was just perfect physically. And I felt every word out of his mouth was totally thought out, totally precise, there were no random things coming out of Peter's mouth, that it was all scripted, but in a very poetic way.

RS: Was there a lot of the word play and the deconstruction that we heard later on, at that time?

LJ: Yeah, and it rose very spontaneously. At the same time, you felt like he must have just spent all of his time thinking up this stuff, and then phrases just appeared, fluently, as if watching a movie. And he didn't need a second take. He was really prepared with all his lines all the time.

RS: And that was true of his music, too, where you've said that he would go to the studio and he'd cut the track and he'd leave. He knew what he wanted, he went in and did it, and left.

LJ: Yeah.

RS: As opposed to Bob, who loved to hang in the studio and jam and work it out, and see how many different versions he could come up with and pick the best. Did Peter do any of that kind of stuff when he recorded? Did he do very radically different versions of his songs, or did he just stick with—

LJ: Not with *Legalize It*. I figured those songs had been in him for so long that he had all the finished versions in his mind, or at least 90 percent. And also we were broke, we didn't have a budget to do that record, and I had to scramble for money to record.

RS: Did you and he become friends immediately? Did he like you?

LJ: I felt that he was accepting of my presence and he treated me with an openness and respect.

RS: Wasn't wary of you? Because he was kind of suspicious about a lot of people.

LJ: No, I never felt that he was suspicious of me at that time. But I think he trusted Bob's instincts about me, which led him to be very open-minded towards me. But I think he felt that my being so close to Bob meant that there must be a real purpose for me being there.

RS: That's very Rasta, isn't it?

LJ: Yes. And that Jah had put me there for this reason and Bob understood that, 'cause Bob was close to me, and he would come to understand that in his time. He wasn't suspicious of me—I never felt a vibe like I was an outsider.

RS: Did you jam with him in the early days the way you did with Bob?

LJ: There were times occasionally in the little rehearsal studio at 56 Hope Road, but it wasn't like with Bob who I jammed with every day.

RS: Or with Bunny?

LJ: No, 'cause Bunny doesn't play anything. I don't know how Bunny writes. He plays a little bit of guitar, but he doesn't sit around jamming.

RS: In the early days it was said that Bunny was not terribly fond of white people.

LJ: Right, but, well, he had this black militancy thing, and Bunny was definitely the most suspicious and paranoid of the three of them. But I had a tremendous relationship with Bunny, and when I started to grow dreadlocks I was spending a lot of time with him, I'd see Bunny almost every day. I would go with Skill and Bob every morning to Bull Bay. We'd run on the beach, run up the mountain to Cane River to the Falls—

RS: That's where you shot those home movies?

LJ: Yeah, and after that I would have breakfast with Bunny.

RS: How was Bunny living at that point, in a house, a hut?

LJ: A hut.

Contemplating the magnificent foliage. >

Peter rarely smoked a spliff unless it was one rolled with corn trash. He preferred his pipe, which was hand-carved, and he always had it with him.

Peter on a donkey with Sledger, Bob's cousin, on our trip to Westmoreland to shoot the cover for Legalize It. *I loved journeying with Sledger; he seemed to be at home no matter how remote the parts we reached. And he was an immaculate driver. Quick but always in control. I felt he could always avoid disaster, no matter what mortacious abandon we might encounter on what seemed to me incalcuable Jamaican roads. He had a way with strangers—disarming them with his warm, deep-brown eyes and sincere, affable smile. Any trip always seemed brighter for Sledger's presence.*

RS: I've eaten fish with Bunny.

LJ: And he'd make me fish tea every morning, and where Peter would treat me as if I had my reasons for being there, Bunny really embraced me. And he was the first person to call me a Wailer. And when Bunny started to call me a Wailer, then I was in the Wailers. We were at Hope Road behind the house where there was a huge Number 11 mango tree and where we used to cook ital food outside. And Bunny just declared it in front of a whole bunch of dreads, including Skill Cole, Take Life, Frowser, Family Man, Carly, and Bob. Bunny was on his way out and he just pronounced, "Lee Jah-free a Wailers mon." Like it should just be obvious to everyone and I could sense that everyone was happy for me, 'cause Bunny was original Wailers, "the toughest of the toughest," and I could see Bob was pleased because it was he that had brought me this far.

RS: I want to ask you about setting up the Sly Stone tour.

LJ: I did.

RS: According to Joe Higgs, there were only five gigs that were done, before Vegas. That's what he recalls.

LJ: Might have been a few more.

RS: Tell me first how you set it up, who you set it up with, and what you remember of the individual gigs leading up to Vegas. Tell me as much as you can about that.

LJ: All right.

RS: Because people say that Bob Marley blew Sly Stone off the stage every night of the tour.

LJ: That's incorrect. (laughs) That is very far from the truth.

RS: Who did you set the tour up with?

LJ: Chris Blackwell had introduced me to Gary Kurfirst, who had been a kind of music business prodigy, managing a band called Mountain as a teenager and later Talking Heads and others. Chris had given me an office to work out of in New York at Island. Island Records at the time was only one little tiny room in the Capitol Records building. It consisted of me and one other person, who was basically a publisher. So Island Records didn't really exist in the U.S. (although of course it was highly successful in England) except for me. And at the time I thought that that might be a

RS: And he had a New York reputation. He was from New Jersey and people knew about him, there was a lot of word around.

LJ: People didn't really know about him either then. This was the beginning of Springsteen, but the hype had already started, major hype, he was like the most hyped new artist of, period. I mean, they were making him out to be the next Bob Dylan before his first album was released.

RS: "He sees the future of rock 'n' roll," says Jon Landau in Rolling Stone.

LJ: So I took the Catch a Fire—no, this is Catch A Fire, this is before Burnin'

RS: So Max's Kansas City was the spring, not the fall. We're talking what, April, May?

LJ: Right, this is for Catch A Fire. Burnin' hadn't been finished yet.

RS: Was Bunny on tour at that point with them, or was it just Bob and Peter?

LJ: Bunny didn't go.

RS: So it was just Bob and Peter, because one Higgs didn't tour, and the half for Burnin'

LJ: Right, that's correct, Bob and Peter.

RS: Who's on keyboards, Wya?

LJ: Wya.

RS: And family and baby, so he's the piano.

LJ: Yeah, that's correct.

RS: And Max's was some small venue?

LJ: Max's was a big stage place. Max's stayed in the '60s as a place for painters, sculptors, major artists hanging out, and Mickey Ruskin, the guy who owned it, would take work in lieu for bills from the real good ones, so he wound up with this massive collection. He died very young, but when he died he had a collection that because worth millions of dollars. He was trading with everyone from Carl Andre

amazing place.
the '60s as a place
ptors, visual artists
d Mickey Ruskin,
ned it, would trade
od.

Sound check for an outdoor concert at the University of Miami. This was the first gig for Peter with the Word Sound and Power band and coincided with the release of Legalize It, *launching his solo career. We were staying in a dingy motel at the beach but what was memorable was a twenty-two-year old Cuban-American named Jommi, a complete stranger who showed up with a van filled with mangoes, papayas, coconuts, bananas, etc. and a big bag of herb—all loving gifts for this ragamuffin band of dreads. Later I discovered we had some distant connections.*

the avant-garde went to eat hamburgers. Then it started changing because they added another room upstairs, where they started to have groups play in the early '70s.

RS: Tell me the dimensions of that upstairs room.

LJ: It could hold a few hundred people, I guess. Long and narrow, like a long loft type of thing. Maybe 250, 300 capacity. It was tight. But when they started to run groups, the whole atmosphere at Max's started to change. It was no longer a place for just artists, although artists could still go there, it was still okay, but it was no longer the place for artists to go. It became the place where glam rock started. The New York Dolls started at Max's. You'd have David Bowie when he was in New York, you'd have all the people from the Warhol movies, all the transvestites—Holly Woodlawn, Jackie Curtis.

RS: It was the very embodiment of what Chris Blackwell told Bunny Wailer he wanted to put him in, and the reason Bunny quit the group. It was a "freak club."

LJ: That's not why Bunny quit the group.

RS: That's what he tells everyone.

LJ: Because of Max's Kansas City?

RS: No, no, because he didn't want to play "freak clubs," and Blackwell told them that the Wailers were "no body," and he says, "Well, I know a body is something that is cold and dead, and we are not bodies, and we don't play for freak clubs." It'll be in his book.

LJ: Well, Max's was a freak club, but it was much more than a freak club. I mean you might have had Holly Woodlawn and Jackie Curtis, but you also had people like Todd Rundgren, Patti Smith, and Lou Reed, all kinds of brilliant people hanging out there.

RS: Trendsetters.

LJ: Yeah, yeah. So it had that kind of atmosphere at that time, it had the glam scene. It started to become a rock star place. You couldn't

get into Max's anymore. You had to be somebody just to walk in. It wasn't what Studio 54 was later, it wasn't this huge place and bouncers. It wasn't that. It was as if there was this mysterious wall, where unless you had a certain sensibility (there weren't any bouncers there) you just couldn't really get inside. It was like the invisible shield. So it became very much a rock-and-roll kind of superstar-type of place.

RS: Tell me about opening night.

LJ: Well, getting there first. I had arranged with this immigration lawyer, but the work permits didn't come in time. But it had become crucial that we make it, because it was a real coup to have these dates opening for Springsteen. But not everything was in order. So this immigration lawyer knew a person that worked at immigration in Niagara Falls. And he worked a certain shift, like four to twelve or something. And we flew to Toronto from Kingston. The idea was to drive to Niagara Falls when this guy was on duty, 'cause he was going to let us in. But, of course, what happens is, we arrive in Toronto and we looked like we were going to overthrow the government. And they went through every piece of luggage. They took hours and hours and hours. So by the time we got to Niagara Falls it was two o'clock in the morning.

RS: So you missed your guy!

LJ: So now I got the lawyer's number at home and woke him up, and he woke up the immigration guy to come, and it was like four o'clock in the morning, and that's how we got into America.

RS: Was this the day before the gig? Did you have any margin in between?

LJ: Yeah, it was like the next day we were supposed to be starting at Max's.

RS: And you're up all night. And it's a hell of a long drive from Niagara Falls to New York City, it's at least eight hours.

LJ: Yeah, it was a long drive, and we had a couple of station wagons.

RS: So they must have been wrecked by the time they got to do the gig.

LJ: Yeah, and where did we stay? Of course, I booked us into the

Chelsea Hotel. I mean, where were we going to stay looking the way we looked? If we didn't have herb to smoke, everybody's going to be really pissed off at me.

RS: So you needed a congenial management.

LJ: Everyone was expecting me to have the herb situation under control. I wasn't in the band yet, this was kind of a beginning for me. And I was Bob's new best friend, and everybody was kind of accepting me and liking me, but, you know, I was responsible for getting them there. I was the reason they were there, and that was where I lived, I was from there. And when I was in Jamaica I always had herb to smoke, and now it's my turn! So where was I going to put them? I had to put them in some place where we could smoke herb. And there was only one hotel, and it happened to be close enough to Max's, it was pretty close, you know, you could jump in a cab and be there in three mintues. So we stayed at the Chelsea Hotel, where Viva lived, where Warhol shot *Chelsea Girls—*

RS: Leonard Cohen. The east coast Chateau Marmont.

LJ: But even more, lots more. So we checked into the Chelsea.

The Chelsea Hotel

Well, this couldn't have been anyone's idea of a five-star hotel, although there were lots of paintings on the walls of the lobby, some of which looked like art, including a Larry Rivers painting of a Dutch Masters cigar ad, which is still there today. The rooms had a shabbiness which bordered on dingy. The paint was ancient and corrupt and peeling in various places, old tarnished fixtures and doorknobs, cracked tiles, everything kind of turn-of-the-century with a morning-after flavor.

But there were other factors weighing in which

Peter with Robbie Shakespeare in the background and Al Anderson at the sound check at the University of Miami. This was the live American debut of Sly and Robbie and the beginning of the international phase of a multifaceted career of touring, recording, and producing that has become legendary. The consummate reggae rhythm masters.

Peter and me at the sound check for the Peace Concert, Kingston, Jamaica 1978.

made the Chelsea Hotel the best choice of lodging for the Wailers' first live dates on their first-ever U.S. tour. It was close to Max's Kansas City, it was relatively inexpensive, and I was able to make a good package deal with Stanley, the thin, hyper-curious owner, for our half-dozen or so rooms. Some of the rooms had kitchens, and since we'd be staying in New York for more than a week it would enable us to cook Jamaican food, especially ital food, which was hard to come by in Manhattan. Most important, since the hotel had been the set for *Chelsea Girls,* which had the scene with Bridget Polk shooting up speed through her jeans, I knew we would not be treated as particularly strange—dreadlocks never having been seen in these parts before—and I knew no one would bother us for smoking herb. The Chelsea Hotel for me was familiar ground and repre-sented safeness, like a womb inside the belly of the beast the dreads called "Babylon."

Looking "forward in reverse" (Family Man had explained to me that "Rasta never goes back"), I can't help thinking I brought dreadlocks to America. I mean, *The Harder They Come* had been released at the same time, but that was a movie. I brought

live dreadlocks in 3D, the dreads from another planet, and where we landed was West Twenty-third Street, the Chelsea, the fortress of the bohemian, where you could sit in the lobby for any given fifteen min-utes on any given day and see maybe Patti Smith and then John Cage followed by Trash stars, transvestites Holly Woodlawn and Jackie Curtis parading phantasmagorically in and out; poets, junkies, playwrights, and thieves, murderers, rock stars, and panhandlers

Jacob Miller. Lead singer for Inner Circle at National Stadium, Kingston, Jamaica, at the sound check for the One Love Peace Concert, planned to help quell tribal war between rival ghetto gangs. Jacob's performance that night was thrilling. The band had a new contract with Island Records and was primed for an interna-tional breakthrough, with a tour scheduled as opening act for the Wailers. I drove with Jacob on the way to the sound check that day, and his driving was so reckless I threatened to get out of the car and walk if he didn't slow down. Late that year he died in a crash, an immeasurable loss to reggae music.

feathered and sequined, not being able to tell one from the other. Where a year later Billy Mainard from the eighth floor, the frail, effeminate pot dealer who would bring us buds and who we would guest list, would be bludgeoned to death in his own room by a total stranger he had picked up on the street, and where several years later the bass player from the Sex Pistols (a group Bob greatly admired), Sid Vicious, would kill his wife, Nancy, and then take his own life.

But our vibe transcended, and by the end of the week we were doing two shows a night and three on the weekend—we were no longer a mild curiosity in a tower of freaks but rather the awesome light of the metropolitan underground. By week's end word had spread and our sets were packed, people coming specifically to see us and leaving before the headliner went on.

And, yeah, we'd cook. I'd go with Bob on foot through the West Side streets to pick fruits from the small corner markets to juice in the blender we had borrowed from my parents on a ride up to their suburban Mt. Kisco house. We'd get rice and peas and vegetables, and Carly, our drummer, would make ital stew, and I would tape the shows, and we'd blast them back through our newly acquired boomboxes—spoils of our victorious march—echoing through the palace halls, honing our sets, making them sharper and richer with each succeeding night.

And I presented to Bob a fair Danish princess, an extraordinary

Sly Dunbar at National Stadium, Kingston, Jamaica, at the sound check for the One Love Peace Concert.

and fragile beauty named Mooskie—with the whitest ivory skin and steel-blue eyes, lithe and nearly as tall as he—who resided on the eleventh floor of the tower after having left her boyfriend,

141

I was tired of the Ovation Peter was playing so when he signed his Columbia contract I took him to West Forty-eighth Street in New York, a whole block of instrument stores, where we found this beautiful cream-colored late-'50s Les Paul. Mr. Touch was entering a new world.

Pete Tosh, Donald Kinsey, Sly Dunbar(drums) and Robbie Shakespeare, Live in Jamaica.

Robbie Shakespeare.

Playing harmonica with Peter Tosh at the Beacon Theater, New York City, 1977.
Photographs by Anton Mikofsky.

Françiose de Menil, the filmmaker who had shot a film for me called *Mask* with a high-speed camera at four thousand frames per second—one shot at an oblique angle of my face in dead silence and black and white—and then the blood-wine erupting in the slowest of motion from my lips and throat and gut over three eternal minutes. (Françiose was the son of the de Menils, the patrons of the arts who started the Dia Art Foundation with the money from royalties from the patent of a particular drill bit used by almost every oil driller on the planet and who supported the great earthworks of De Maria and Heizer), and how ironic, my previous infatuation with death now transformed by Rasta into a rich and visceral love of life eternal.

And Bob glowed around Mooskie, who adored him, knowing that when the week was up she may or may not but caring not and lavishing in the moments flowing like the evening traffic down Seventh Avenue—the sprinkling of headlights at dusk and the sun setting beyond the Hudson River, glowing strange incandescent colors through the toxic gasses spewing from the sprawling Jersey refineries.

And she would take his arm and guide him through the teeming concrete corridors and Bob's smile thrilling with his prize and I would join them, Mooskie leading through the red, gold, and green October of Central Park and on to the lavish prewar apartments of my herb-dealing friends, the intractable search for the better draw where inevitably the sounds from the best stereos would be blasting *Catch A Fire*. And for this eventful week we owned the soul of the cultural epicenter of the Western world and began to transform profoundly and irrevocably the heart of popular music everywhere on Jah's earth.

RS: Did the Wailers each have a separate room at the Chelsea?

LJ: No. But I think Bob and Peter had single rooms.

RS: All right, now take me to the club on opening night.

LJ: We used to cop herb from Billy Mainard. He was really funny, and he had good herb. I had friends who were herbsmen in the city too, and they would bring us herb.

RS: Was it sensi yet?

LJ: No, we were smoking Colombian herb that had seeds in it. And we tried to get the red ones, red or gold. But it was all Colombian. They didn't even have sensi in Jamaica yet. And so it was okay.

RS: And did Bob meet Springsteen at that time?

LJ: Not at the sound check. Bob didn't really care about Springsteen. He would have been impressed to meet Curtis Mayfield.

RS: Did they not ever sit through any of Springsteen's sets?

LJ: Yeah, because we were there. What were we going to do? We were playing two sets a night and three on the weekend.

RS: They didn't care for his music?

LJ: I don't think it was that they didn't care for it. I thought they thought he was good enough—

RS: —to be on the same bill with them?

LJ: (laughs) No, it wasn't like that. It was just like wide-eyed, you know, this was like another world. I mean, we were all of a sudden right in the center of the heart of rock and roll glamourdom.

RS: The epicenter of hipness.

Our cook, Biggs, Al Anderson and Peter waiting for the plane on the Legalize It *tour.*

LJ: Without a doubt. This was it. This was the place in the world, the hippest place in the world you could possibly play, opening for Bruce Springsteen at his first Columbia Records show. I mean, everybody who was anybody was there that week. I mean, more than once. We were playing two shows a night, and this was the kind of thing where

A morning spliff at Peter's place in Spanish Town, getting ready to go to Kingston for the recording of Legalize It.

people came more than once. Every writer, everybody from the fashion world, every musician that meant anything who was in New York had to go see this. And we were there, and by the end of the week everybody knew who we were. And it wasn't like Sly and the Family Stone where we just played and everybody just sat there. We were blowing people's minds! People were flipping out over us. I mean, it was incredible. We were getting amazing respect—it started the love affair of the press with the Wailers that week. And it never ended.

RS: Were there any Jamaicans there in the audience that week?

LJ: No, no.

RS: That's not the kind of club they would go to normally.

LJ: The invisible shield at Max's! (laughs) And you couldn't get in these dates. This place was small. You could not get in. You have to realize Columbia Records bought all the seats. You couldn't even get into Max's anyway, just to go have a hamburger. And then, to get upstairs to see Bruce Springsteen, I mean forget about it! This was the major event of the year in the music world, these Springsteen dates.

RS: (Reading from bootleg cassette label of one of the Max's dates.) "Put It On," "Slave Driver," "Burning and Looting," "Stop That Train," "Kinky Reggae," "Stir It Up," that's a set from Max's Kansas City.

LJ: What about "Midnight Ravers"?

RS: Well, that's all I have. I've never found any more than this one.

RS: Tell me about Peter's first tour [in the summer of 1977] and the Cuban at the Miami motel.

LJ: We were staying at some dive motel in South Beach before it was "South Beach," twenty years before. Although the Wailers were huge stars in the press, it had only been recently with the *Natty Dread* album that anything had reached 100,000 in sales. Before that nothing reached 10,000 in sales, and even *Natty Dread* was far from a commercial hit. Although Peter signed with Columbia

Records, the biggest record company in the world at the time, they were treating this tour like we were just some other band they had signed, who couldn't support themselves on the road. So we were just staying at the cheapest places we could tolerate. This guy shows up, a perfect stranger with a van filled to the gills with papayas, mangoes, all tropical fruits, bananas, coconuts, this big bag of really nice herb. And this just gave us inspiration to do this tour.

RS: The Marvin Gaye concert in 1974 found you onstage with the Wailers. What do you remember?

LJ: It was at the Carib Theatre, which held about 2,500 people. What it really was, was a big Marvin Gaye event. At the time he was at the height of his worldwide popularity, and in Jamaica they are very picky about what kind of American music they like, and Marvin Gaye was special. A lot of his popularity had to do with the social and political themes of the songs on the *What's Goin' On* album. He showed up in Jamaica with a seventy-piece orchestra. It was a really big event, a hot ticket. The promoter added the Wailers onto the show, but nobody really believed they would play, because they hadn't played in Jamaica in many years and several previous shows had falsely advertised the Wailers. The reason we played the show was that everyone was just swept up in the vibe. There was a new Wailers single out and it was a smash and we felt we wouldn't be overshadowed by Marvin, that even with his huge crew he couldn't upstage us. And that proved to be true.

What was exciting for me, particularly, was that we had just put out "Road Block" and it was a massive hit. It was a number one record and it featured my harmonica playing, and I knew that we would have to do that song, and there was no way that the Wailers could do that song without me getting up there and playing on it, because I'm playing from the intro on. And just having the harmonica on a reggae track was such a novelty, the novelty aspect definitely contributed to the record having such immediate popularity. Of course, most important was the lyrical content of that song, because there were road blocks anywhere, anytime, and it was particularly difficult for people like us dreadlocks, because there's no way that we would be caught in a road block and the police just saying that you could go. And since we smoked herb all the time, we were living in a world that hovered between total apprehension and a heightened state of all-encompassing fear. So I remember being very anxious that whole day. First of all, none of the Wailers were really quite sure if we were going to play. It was going to be the kind of thing

where Bunny and Peter would show up at Hope Road, because it was Bob, Bunny, and Peter who would have to decide. And there'd be some kind of reasoning as to, "Are we going to get this together?" and if the vibe was right, there was an outside chance that it just might happen. The whole town was buzzing over Marvin Gaye's appearance. It seemed like all this buzz over him in some way took some of the pressure off us, and we're paying some kind of tribute to, or acknowledgment of, Marvin by showing up there. And at the same time it was a matter of playing when the Wailers hadn't played Jamaica in a long time, and being that we were just opening for this big event that this show had become, there wouldn't be so much focus of attention on us. I remember Peter and Bunny showing up separately in the morning, and it was just kind of the vibe of let's do it. So I was all excited, because I knew what that meant. I was going to have to get out there. We have the number one song, and I'm playing on it, and it's totally political, about the police busting you for herb, and I'm going to be onstage with the whole consciousness of the island focused on these twenty to thirty feet. And the show ends up megapacked, because the place only held 2,500 people, and there were thousands of people who couldn't get in. This show could have drawn 20 to 30,000 people easily. So the Wailers come out, they play like five songs, and the audience is totally loving it, and I'm on the side of the stage, and I know they gotta play it, because everybody's waiting for it. And I remember I was standing with Skill Cole and it was my time, and he just kind of pushed me out there and said, "You gotta go now," he gave me a little shove, and I was out onstage with the lights blaring at me. My

locks were really big by then, I had a red tam, I definitely looked like I was in the Wailers, except that I was white. And Bob says into the microphone, "This is Lee..." and it flashes through my mind that Bob Marley is introducing me to Jamaica and then he finishes the sentence with an instruction to the engineer, "Don't turn him up too loud." And the audience is cracking up and then the first few notes of the intro and then I come in wailing and the place goes completely crazy. And I'm playing through the rest of the song and my nervousness is dissolving and I'm the highest I've ever been in my life until then, and then I have this big solo that kind of went on and on and I'm trading riffs with lead guitarist Al Anderson through the outro and it's sounding really good and I'm starting to feel like I passed the test. And it was totally thrilling. It was a coming forward for me. It was like I had been accepted by everybody in the band already, otherwise I wouldn't have been out there at that moment, no way, and this was kind of like the band presenting me, and the audience was so electric. The fact that

they had just done five songs, the place was going crazy already before I came out kind of eased the pressure, because I just walked into the environment that was already totally scintillating. My nervousness disappeared, dissolved, and I was kind of just lost in the music, trying not to step on Bob's vocals or I knew I'd be in a lot of trouble. I would never get the chance to go out there again. But it was good. By the time it got further down the song to my solo, I was just rocking with it. And I think I did a good job on the solo. And twenty-six years later I finally got to hear a tape of that perfor-

mance, and the solo does sound pretty good. And of course the great thing about it was that after that I was just in the Wailers. Although it was a few months earlier, I believe, that Bunny had pronounced while he was at Hope Road, "Lee is Wailers," being on stage was still definitely an initiation. And being part of the group obviously was more than being in a band. It meant that I was accepted into the whole cultural, spiritual, political context which being in this band implied. I could be on the street in downtown Kingston and I was no longer a curiosity, I was now an accepted part of the fraternity of musicians—and more: I was Wailers.

Don Taylor was a valet for Marvin Gaye and a real fast talker, and he seemed well connected, because he was with Marvin and it was all very grandiose having the seventy-piece orchestra traveling to this Caribbean island.

Donald Kinsey. His father is the legendary blues man Big Daddy Kinsey, and he has a group with his brothers, the Kinsey Report. He grew up outside Chicago in Gary, Indiana, where regular visitors to his home included Muddy Waters and Albert King. Donald was a child prodigy, performing as a pre-teen. By the time he was sixteen he was Albert King's band leader.

Marvin certainly was one of the biggest stars in popular music at that time and Bob was managerless. I had been performing a lot of management-type duties, but I certainly wasn't inclined to be anyone's manager. Especially because performing that function for Bob and the band was a fulltime job, and it just wasn't anything I aspired to. I don't know if I would have been good at it anyway. I was searching for someone to do

Donald Kinsey, the great American blues guitarist who I brought to Jamaica to play with Peter, at Sheila Bay just outside Ocho Rios on the north coast.

it, but I didn't really know anybody. I had a friend in Miami who was an herb dealer named Robbie Yuckman and later on he helped finance the *Legalize It* album, joking that if it was ultimately successful in what it was trying to do, it would put him out of business. He was a friend from college, tough but kindhearted and generous. He had a lot of money, and I felt it would take a lot of money to manage the Wailers, and I tried to convince him to do it. He kind of toyed with the idea a little bit, but I don't know if he would have

been really good at it. He came to Jamaica around the time of the Marvin Gaye show. He talked to Bob, but I think he kind of felt that this was going to be an enormous amount of work and could possibly be a thankless job. So his enthusiasm waned, and I didn't really know any managers unfortunately. And the band really needed someone. *Natty Dread* was being finished. Until then, there was no money to be made. The first two albums, *Catch A Fire* and *Burnin'*, hadn't

Auntie. Bob's aunt, on the porch of the house at Nine Mile, St. Ann's Parish, Jamaica, where Bob was born.

sold. There was no money to be made on gigs. So the truth is, whatever managers I might have been able to find probably wouldn't have taken the job, because there was no income. So, in stepped Don Taylor, who appeared to be in the right place at the right time. He was born and grew up in Jamaica, so he could relate to Bob pretty well and he seemed to have all these connections. He was an incredibly fast talker, cut from the record business promotion-man classic mold, not unlike Bob's previous manager, Danny Sims. Still, everything at that time was uncharted territory.

Donald Kinsey(r) with Jack Ruby at Jack Ruby's house in Ocho Rios. Jack produced many reggae classics, including the great early records of Burning Spear.

Bob had a new Island Records extension, and in some respects things looked promising. On the other hand, there was still a question of whether we could really sell any records. I'm sure Taylor used the race card. I was really skeptical of him. I didn't trust him from the beginning. I was sure Bob could do better. So we were immediately at odds. But once Bob decided to go with him, my role changed. My only responsibility from then on was to play harmonica, and in a way, that was a big relief. Because I was feeling all the financial burden that Bob was carrying. For myself, it was easy because I didn't have any kids, I was single, I was used to living without any money. In fact, it was a political stance to live without money.

The band was really poor. Bob had lots of kids. Family Man was going on fifteen kids or something by then, and Bob didn't have a manager, and Chris Blackwell was probably hoping they would find a competent manager because he was going very far out on a limb, considering that the first two albums hadn't sold, and here he was paying for a third one. By committing to this third album he was also committing to a new tour, which was definitely going to be more expensive than the previous ones, because now there were more people in the band with the "I Three." So although I was really disappointed with Bob going with Don Taylor as manager, it was also a big relief for me, not having to be a main link to the outside business world.

Legendary session player Cornell Dupree recording with Joe Cocker at Dynamic studio, Kingston, Jamaica, 1976.

Jacob Miller at 56 Hope Road.

Joe Cocker, Terra Nova Hotel, Kingston, Jamaica, 1976. He was in Jamaica recording an album with the legendary R&B session players Richard Tee, Cornell Dupree, Steve Gad, and Eric Gale. I knew the producer, and he asked me if I could get the Wailers to do a song, as Joe wanted to have a reggae track on the album. The idea was to do a reggae version of the Bob Dylan song "The Man in Me." I asked Family Man, Carly, and Peter if they wanted to do it, and they agreed. Joe, who was alcoholic, was very nervous about meeting them, and sadly, when the 7:00 PM start time approached, Joe had drunk himself into unconsciousness and never got to meet them, although they laid the track for him to voice-over later.

Yvonne. Peter Tosh's girlfriend who died from injuries sustained in a car accident in which Peter was driving. Peter blamed himself and never recovered from the psychological wounds.

Karl Pitterson. Brilliant engineer and producer who mixed the Legalize It *album and went on to produce the first two Steel Pulse albums as well as many others.*

Island album, and everyone was pissed off at Blackwell for the previous albums not selling, even though Chris had treated the Wailers as a major priority, Bob had asked me to explore finding another possible label. Right at that time, the Grateful Dead were starting their own label, and that was the early '70s, when the Dead were huge, at the zenith of their popularity. And in a lot of ways they embodied much of the revolutionary spirit that the Wailers did. So, I thought that it might be a possibility, signing with them. And I got in touch with Bill Graham, and it turned out the band were big fans and they were really into the idea, and they flew Bob and me out to San Francisco for a Grateful Dead concert at the Fillmore, where they were playing for a week. Obviously it sold out every night. And we went there and we sat in the first row of the balcony with Bill Graham. It was pretty incredible, and they rolled out the red carpet for us. We went backstage, they took us out to dinner, they had the best herb for us to smoke. They treated us like royalty. They loved us, they were major Wailers fans. They were ready to do whatever it took. They promised to take us on tour with them, which meant we'd be

Donald Kinsey

playing for tens of thousands of people every night. A Grateful Dead tour in those days was an amazing event. It was definitely an audience that would buy Wailers records. It would have meant going from selling two thousand albums to hundreds of thousands of albums guaranteed. But Bob wasn't always the one to go the easy way. He backed out because they were called the Grateful Dead. There wasn't really any other reason. I didn't have a reply to Bob concerning the Grateful Dead because I was just this new Rasta myself. I think Bob wasn't wrong, really, because the Grateful Dead was a concept. The irony is that Jerry Garcia lived several years past Bob. But it was the Rasta concept of eternal life, Rasta didn't believe in death, that completely changed my life around and that's why I am alive today. So, I really couldn't disagree with Bob about the Dead's lifestyle. Jerry Garcia was a junkie, and the reason he died as young as he did was that he didn't take care of his body. And in the Rasta world, the body is the temple of the Lord and has to be respected. And I had just come to this realization from being among Rasta, and I couldn't argue with Bob on this point. It seemed very visceral, very intrinsic in the whole Dead thing. We were about life. They were about death. So how could the Wailers be touring with the Grateful Dead, we were the grateful living. The Dead represented many things that I had left behind. Although in a lot of ways it seemed like a good fit for us politically, the spiritual side seemed too far away to find a bridge for that wide a gulf. Bob liked their offer, he was flattered by it. I made him understand really clearly how it would work for us economically and he really considered it back in 1974.

Bill Graham would have been their manager. I don't know whether that would have been better or not. In the end, it's really about the music. And I think the music Bob made after that is incredible. Bob grew musically, and it's a credit to Chris Blackwells' genius that he understood his music better than any other music executive could have. With Chris, he had a collaborator who helped him thrive creatively. So you can't really say it would have been better. How could it have been better than *Survival*? Would it have meant that Bob would have lived longer? No, I don't think so. Who knows? Only Jah.

Robbie Shakespeare outside Channel One Studio, Kingston, Jamaica. Robbie didn't smoke herb, but he had his picture taken with this spliff. After six months of persistence, I had just convinced him to do the Legalize It *tour. It meant giving up his job doing sessions at Channel One, where he would start at eight in the morning and go late into the night, playing on ten, twelve tracks a day for ten dollars a track. He and Sly were on all the hits. In those days, ten Jamaican dollars was the equivalent of ten U.S. dollars, and I could only offer him two hundred dollars a week for the tour.*

When the *Natty Dread* tour came about, Taylor didn't like me around because I was the only American there, along with Al, and Al didn't like Don Taylor that much either. So I think Taylor was paranoid about our being around, and especially me. He figured if he could get rid of me, he could probably deal with Al. I was only playing on a few songs, so what was the big deal? He was trying to get me to leave, he was treating me really badly. The thing that was really annoying about Don Taylor was that he really saw himself as the star of the band, as equal to Bob. In fact, what he used to do, during shows, he would stand onstage, often in front of band members. He particularly liked to stand in front of Al. When I got

Alan "Skill" Cole

onstage to play, he'd always try to stand in front of me. So I was reaching a crossroads about what I was going to do with my life, because it wasn't enough for me to be a harmonica player on a few songs. I had done that. And here was the manager of the band not wanting me there. And so, I made up my mind to leave after the New York date of the Natty Dread tour,

Marcia Griffiths

which was about two-thirds of the way through [in summer 1975]. I was loving playing. Some of the shows were unforgettable. Just the thrill of being onstage with the Wailers on tour, with them as a member of their band night after night, I viewed as a great accomplishment in my life, and I still do. An unforgettable time. The thrill of being up there with the audience responding the way they were responding then was truly ennobling. I was a member of the greatest band in the world.

Keith Richards jamming at his house above Ocho Rios on the north coast of Jamaica.

RS: Tell me about the fight you had with Bob. Where was it?

LJ: I was in a motel room, mid-1974, and it was the kind of a fight where you throw a couple of punches, but you don't really want to punch the person, so it turns into a wrestling match. Basically it was over the album cover. Me, not only did I not get credit for playing on the record, or any songwriting contributions, but other people got credit for things they didn't even participate in. We were in L.A. and had just seen the album cover at the Island Records' office, which was a converted residential house on Sunset Boulevard in Hollywood. The thing that was most disturbing is that when we saw the cover, they had changed *Knotty Dread* to *Natty Dread*. I protested that they had spelled the title of the album incorrectly, but Bob said nothing to back me up. I was stunned. When we got back to the motel, I wanted to know if he was going to let the album come out like that, and he started to go off on me about how I was too concerned about my own credit, but I wasn't buying it. I wanted to know how the album that was called *Knotty Dread* could be released with a title that meant exactly the opposite. It turned into us cursing at each other. It started with shoving, but I wasn't going to back down. And then it turned into a fist fight. We were about the same size. Nobody really won. It just ended in exhaustion, but it wasn't really over, because nothing had been resolved. We stopped talking to each other and it wasn't till what a year later when I was in jail in Kingston Central, and Bob was off the island, when he arranged for me to have money for a lawyer that I was able to forgive him, knowing that his being there for me was more important than any guilt we could possibly have... For me it wasn't the same anymore between us because part of my desire to go play with Peter came from the fact that I felt I had contributed so much to *Knotty Dread* without any credit. It kind of put me in the same boat with Peter. We both had something to prove with *Legalize It*.

We both had something to prove with *Legalize It.*

" You see men sailing on their ego trips… Blast off on their space ship. Million miles from reality No care for you, no care for me…"

– BOB MARLEY

The photographs in this section were digitally captured from archival video shot by Lee Jaffe, some of which were hand colored by Geoff Gans, summer 2002.

I reminded myself of what Bob had told me, "You can't lost in Jamaica." I supposed what he meant by that was: it was an island. No matter, hours, days weeks, years, you're bound to wind up on the coast. "Can't lost in Jamaica, mon."

I was determined to get to New York. I wasn't going to leave before getting to the gig in Central Park, outdoors, before my friends and family. I wasn't going to miss that. That was a major event for me. And after the Central Park show that night I was at a friend's bar on the Upper East Side called Dr. Generosity's, where a lot of musicians used to hang out. I went there with Al, and there was this gorgeous girl, part African, part Chinese, part white, and she was staring at us, and I was sure she was into Al. I said to Al, "This girl is so gorgeous, you got to go over there, she's staring at you, she's incredible." I insisted, so he goes over to her and talks to her, and he comes back and says, "She's been staring at you, man." I couldn't believe it. And I go over to her and before I can say anything she says to me, "Was that you playing the harmonica with the Wailers today?" And from that day, for the next four years, she was my girlfriend. She was Jamaican, twenty-two years old, and had been living in New York for ten years. Her father had been the Attorney General of Jamaica and her mother was one of the directors of the World Bank. She had this amazing family. She was in college in New York, and I felt meeting her was a reward that Jah had bestowed upon me for all my hard work. Her name was Madaline Scott, her family owned Noel Coward's former estate on the north coast of Jamaica, near Port Maria, called Blue Harbour. I'm still friends with the family, and when I go to Jamaica today I still stay at Blue Harbour. So, Central Park was my last show with Bob, and I decided then to go and work with Peter.

In Jail in Kingston, 1974

This was "Road Block" time, late 1974, and I had to throw away my little herb stalk. I was traveling with Seeco Patterson and my friend Robbie Yuckman, who I had enticed to come down to Jamaica to possibly manage the band. We went up to the mountains in St. Ann's and came back with a little bit of herb and some pollen in a kind of powder form, which is what you can press to make hash. We got stopped in a road block at night about 3 o'clock, coming into Kingston. First they took us into the police station to book us and somehow Seeco just managed to walk away. We're talking late at night, Seeco just kind of dissolved into the darkness. And I was quite relieved because I was afraid they would be harsh on him, being he was a sufferer. That left me and Robbie and I immediately told the police when they were booking us that the stash was mine, he had nothing to do with it, and I was the one who wound up being arrested. They took me to Kingston Central, an infamous jail in downtown Kingston. It was the middle of the night, and it was pretty scary. When I walked into the jail, you could look down from some of the cells through a kind of courtyard that you could walk through, and I hear somebody shouting my

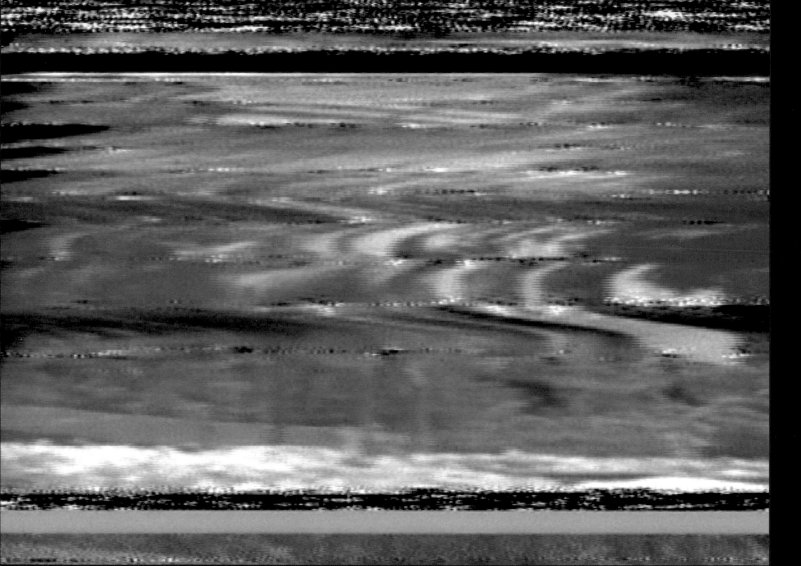

name. And I look up, and it's Bucky Marshall, who was at the time the most infamous gunman in Jamaica, and someone who used to hang out with the Wailers a lot and considered me his spar, his good friend. From when I saw Bucky a lot of the fear that was gripping me dissolved because I knew from Bucky acknowledging me that no one was going to mess with me. They put me in a cell called Big Five, where they throw all the immediate detainees. There were twenty-three people in this room that night, about ten feet square, so it was impossible to lie down. We were just all cramped and squashed, but at least I was protected.

The unfortunate part was that it wasn't looked upon as just a little herb. Since it was in powder form nobody wanted to say what it was. And they had one chemist who worked for the police, and he was on vacation, so I was stuck in this jail until they could determine that this was cannabis. And this guy was gone for a week.

I remember distinctly there was this huge guy who had been Caribbean heavyweight boxing champion who was a prisoner, and he

was extremely articulate, and he had the job of cleaning up the passageway outside the cells and he got to converse with all the prisoners. He began to engage me in conversation. He was quite brilliant and had read all of Franz Fanon and lots of philosophy and anthropology. And at night we'd hear these screams sometimes and this is where Bucky really saved me, because he turned me on to the fact that this guy was in jail for being a rapist. The screams were coming from him raping people—he'd take people out of the cells, and I would have for sure been easy prey for this guy because he could have easily talked me into getting out of the cell, and then I would have been trapped, and I would have been one of those people screaming. So I always felt like Bucky had nearly, if not actually, saved my life. And I was forever indebted to him for warning me and protecting me, and I was later extremely sad to hear that he was gunned down in a war among rival posses.

Bob was off the island. This is after the release of *Natty Dread*. We had just had this big fight in L.A. over the *Natty Dread* cover, and we hadn't talked in a few months. The fight was really bitter. But when

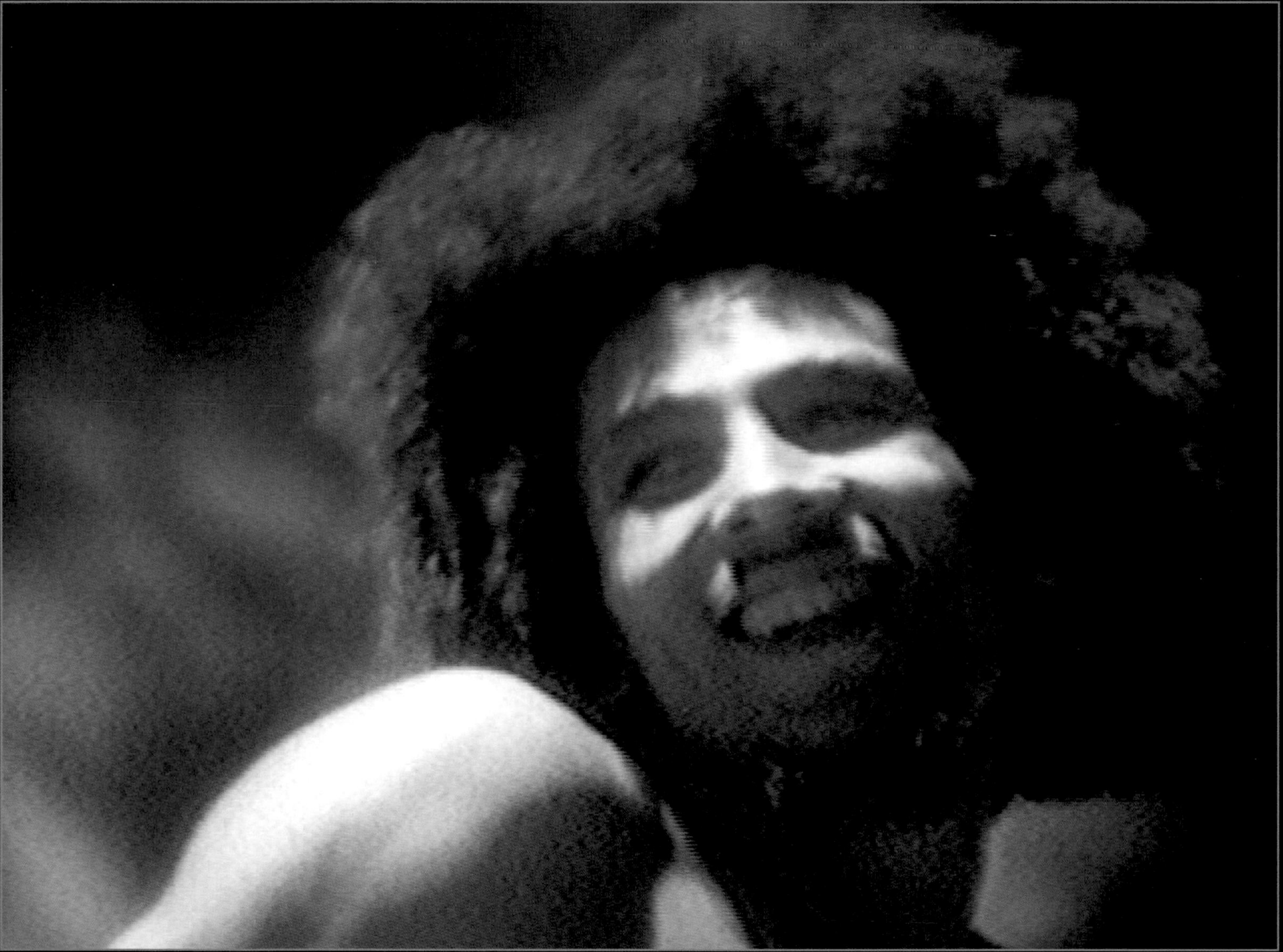

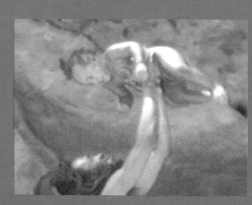  

Ras Daniel Hartman with his son at Cane River Falls outside Kingston Jamaica. Daniel had just co-starred with Jimmy Cliff in Perry Henzell's The Harder They Come.

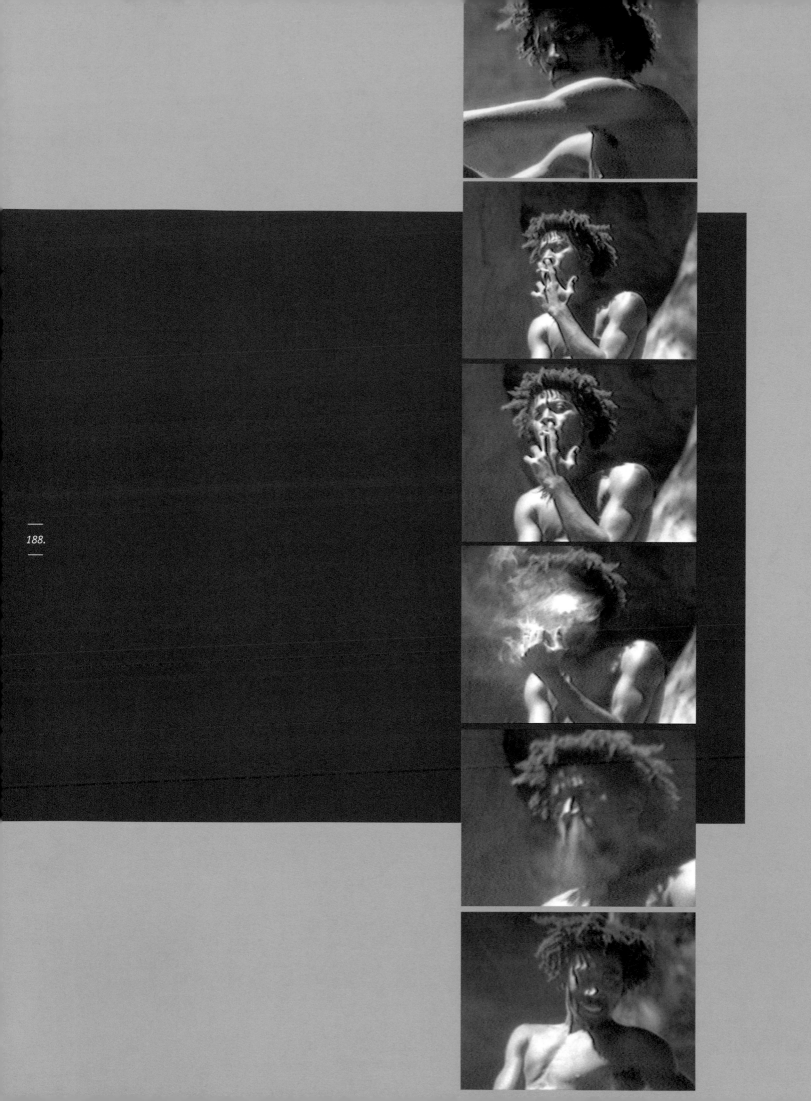

Bunny Wailer. Jamaica, 1973.

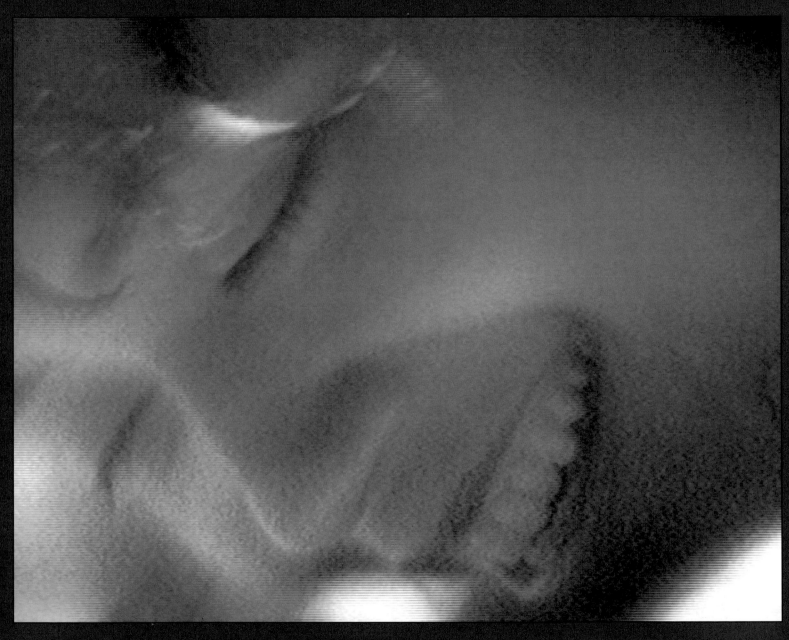

Esther Anderson. Jamaica, 1973.

Bob heard I was in jail, he made sure that there was money for me to have a lawyer, and Rita either came to the jail or made sure somebody else came with food for me to eat every day. And when it came time for my hearing in court to see what was going to happen to me, quite a number of people showed up to say that I should be allowed to stay on the island, including Rita and Perry Henzell. They let me go, and that was the end of it. I had to pay a fine, and Bob arranged for that to be paid, which made me feel that he was going to be there for me, despite whatever bitter disagreements we might have had, and it just made our bond beyond solid.

Peter Tosh—the making of *Legalize It* (late 1975)

Beads of rain splatter against the Air Jamaica window in the squall. We are descending now. The harbor of Kingston is visible below, oil refineries, oil tankers, a couple of small drenched fishing boats further out. Blue mountains surrounding the city. It is afternoon. I am glad for the rain. Coming into Kingston in the afternoon, the sun beating down. It's a hot proposition.

My mind forwarded in reverse to a week before, the Amtrak from New York to Wilmington, Delaware. The *Natty Dread* tour was over. I had left right after the New York date, somewhere near the end of the tour, in the summer of 1975. It was the last show I would play with Bob Marley. It was a triumphant date, on the one hand. Central Park, my hometown, playing in front of 10,000 people, overflowing the outdoor stands to the rocks behind. A perfect summer day. Not too hot. The crowd was wildly enthusiastic. But I had known earlier that my days playing with Bob were num-

"Seeco" Patterson steps into the Cane River Falls, Jamaica, 1973.

bered. His new manager used to walk onstage and try to stand in front of me when it was time to take a solo. Bob was on a new, and what seemed to me less idealistic, path. The days of innocence were over. And any voice of reason that I might have represented was certainly a danger to his new so-called manager.

There was a feeling of ecstasy and triumph with all those screaming fans, and my family and friends among them. But it was also an appropriate moment to make the split. Peter and Bunny had gone before. I had decided then that I would work with Peter Tosh on what would be his first solo album. I would help him career-wise like I had Bob, but there was also a need for me to have an expanded role creatively. I learned volumes being in the studio for the recording of the *Burnin'* and *Natty Dread* albums, and I knew Peter would be open to my artistic input. I was savoring the challenge of making a landmark album, working directly with Peter from inception to release.

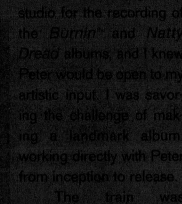

The train was approaching Wilmington, where Ms. B. lived, Mrs. Booker, Bob's mother, with her two kids, Bob's half-brothers. I used to play basketball with the older one, Richard, then ten years old, in the schoolyard across the street from their home.

198.

Arriving in Wilmington, I was never sure if I was in a southern city that looked like the north or a northern city that just moved in slow motion. It felt as if I was in another decade, another era. Semi-dilapidated houses, the neighborhood segregated and black.

The Bookers' house always neat, immaculately clean. Ms. B., tall, robust, outgoing; Mr. Booker thin, frail, quiet. Ms. B. would cook us rice and peas, steam fish. Somehow she was able to find plantains to fry. If not calaloo, at least collard greens. The aroma wafted through my head as the train arrived in the Wilmington station. I knew, no matter what dissension there was between us, our friendship was interminable, and Bob would be there with Mr. Booker, picking me up in a ten-year-old well-oiled Chevy station wagon. Bob, secure with the anticipation that I'd be

arriving with the best spliff that New York had to offer and we'd be eating and playing music like nothing happened. Peter and I were both broke, but I knew that Bob wouldn't deny either of us. I suspected he knew that I was coming to seek his help, and that Peter was probably too proud to ask him himself. The thousand dollars that he gave me on that trip to Wilmington was the beginning of the *Legalize It* album, and Peter's solo career. I had gained Bob's blessing to work with Peter.

The iron bird floated down to Kingston, wheels skidding on the wet runway. I braced myself for the inevitable bombardment of riff-raff, hustlers, ragamuffins, conmen, thieves, herb dealers, dope dealers, money changers, taxi-busmen, minivan racers that were about to descend upon me. Even though I was a dreadlocks, I was still white, fair game. I had only my patois to guard me from the hordes. I made my way past immigration, to the local rent-a-car place, where the manager recognized me. I took the Toyota Corolla and escaped the airport. I stopped past the roundabout to drink two jelly coconuts. Somehow it always felt right drinking some jellies when arriving in Jamdown—the feeling of washing away all the chaos of Babylon with the pure clear water, the irresistible tangy sweetness.

The rain had stopped now, and two jellies weren't enough. I drank two more, and all the people at the bamboo fruit stand laughed to see this white dreadlocks devouring so many of the translucent ital dreadnuts. I laughed with them, gave the Rastaman a five-dollar bill, and was off to town. I hated driving alone. My poor sense of direction—not being sure where to turn—made me feel like a tourist, white and isolated even after years of tracking the same route. I reminded myself of what Bob had told me, "You can't lost in Jamaica." I supposed what he meant by that was: it was an island. No matter, hours, days, weeks, years, you're bound to wind up on the coast. "Can't lost in Jamaica, mon."

The rain was starting and stopping, and the sun was piercing through the clouds. I could see the double rainbow in the rearview mirror, bending over Bull Bay behind me. Ahead of me assorted goats, some on ropes, and children scattering. Buses belching black soot, cars honking, all sorts of mutant cars pieced together, assembled from parts derived from random decades. Taxis sputtering along, occasionally new Benzes. Shanty houses along the road, and this wasn't even the ghetto yet. A sense of desperation. The sense of hopelessness, unemployment. A deadly game of politricks, small favors, gangs of youths converging,

emerging, disentangling, the ragamuffin soldiers hustling along the street corners and the alleys. Disenfranchised teenagers, hoping for what?

The occasional Benzes seemed like armored vehicles impervious to the pain, the interminable suffering—the rudeness—hollow to the despair. Chickens, and an occasional mongoose, skirted across the road. What responsibility had I taken upon my shoulders? What reason for being here? Armed with what? Only my intellect, my ability to suffer as well, intractable. There were moments when doubt overwhelmed me, in turgescent waves. I allowed myself an edgy, ironic smile. "Can't lost in Jamaica, mon."

I turned right. I was going to stop at Harry J's studio uptown. Bob had said that there were three rolls of virgin tape we could use. I thought it best to show up at Peter's with money for studio time and tape, ready to roll. Besides, I needed to stop at Hope Road, which was just around the corner from Harry J's, nyam a mango, and let everyone know I was still alive.

The gateman at Harry J's knew me and waved me through. Bob hadn't called to let them know to give me the tapes. It wasn't necessary. I was probably the one person whose word they could trust, without checking with Bob, to hand me over tapes.

I split to Hope Road. Fifty Six Hope Road was a colonial great house that Chris Blackwell had bought in an upscale part of town with the intention of the Wailers' using it. It had a big yard, and in the back of the yard were the former slave quarters, which we had transformed into a rehearsal studio. There was a giant Number 11 mango tree in the middle of the yard. I could hear music coming from the studio. I knew Fams would be there—"Family Man," the Wailers' bass player, who was also teacher and mentor for young musicians. His unique, innovative style and authorship of brilliant new rhythms directly or indirectly influenced a whole generation of players in Jamaica and far beyond. I think of Fams now struggling financially, decades later, his music the

backbone of records that have sold tens of millions of copies, generated hundreds of millions of dollars of sales—having to eke out a living playing as the remnant of the Wailers.

As I entered I could see Take Life, Frowzer, and Seeco around the iron pot, cooking in the yard, in animated conversation. "What a Raas!" Seeco bawled out with feigned astonishment. "Wha de blood claat, mon? Who de blood claat dat, mon? Gone away and left me, mon? Why you do dat, mon?" Seeco was the Wailers percussionist, but more importantly he was Bob's confidant. He was older, but how old, I could never tell. Maybe thirty-five. Maybe sixty. He was an astute critic of the music, and Bob's link with the blue beat, ska, and mento of the past. He talked in a stutter that was so lyrical it was never annoying. He was decked out in new Adidas—running shoes, sweats—spoils from the Natty Dread tour. I loved Seeco, he was kind, generous, considerate, and I had spent countless hours with him and Bob jamming, Bob on acoustic guitar, Seeco on whatever was available to bang on, me playing harmonica. Seeco always made me feel like I belonged.

From around the fire, Frowzer and Take Life smiled. "Come here Lee Jaffe, mon," said Take Life, putting his arm around me. "Got a spliff fe you, mon. Come here, mon. What you bring me, mon? You bring me a track shoes, mon?" Take Life and Frowzer were youths, sixteen and seventeen years old, who by reputation were among the baddest youths of all the Kingston ghettoes. Take Life was 5'4", light chocolate brown skin, thin frame, and a baby face, with an ingratiating smile that could turn in an instant deadly serious. He had eyes that seemed far older than his days. Frowzer, not more than two inches taller, stockier and darker, the more outgoing of the two, could talk nonstop. They were always clean and nattily dressed, so you could tell they were getting money from somewhere. They were dreadlocked, Frowzer's sticking straight up out of his skull, and they had no reason to push up their chests and act bigger than they were. They were bad, and the outward calm they exuded, though I didn't realize it till much later, came from knowing they were universally feared and were not afraid of dying.

Bob had let them move into Hope Road, saying he was reforming them. I'd wake up in the morning when I was living there and hear them boasting of their escapades of the night before—lootings, shootings, stabbings. Stories that, if I could trust my ears and limited patois, sounded like gang rapes and torture. Surely these were fabrications, kids bragging to each other of how bad they could be. After all, these were my guardian angels, two cherubs that, when I was living there, Bob had assigned to stick

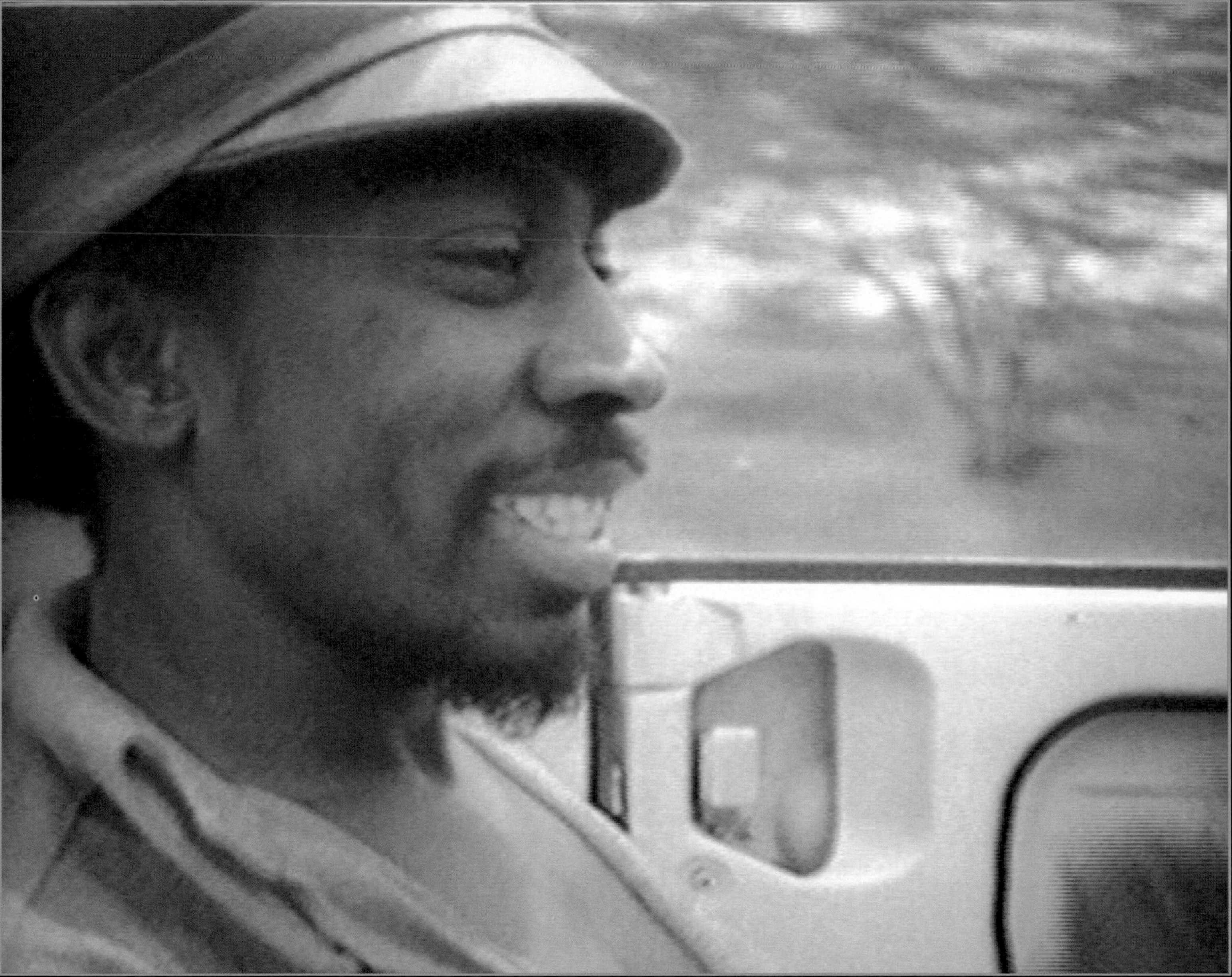

Dusk dissolving, descending into night.

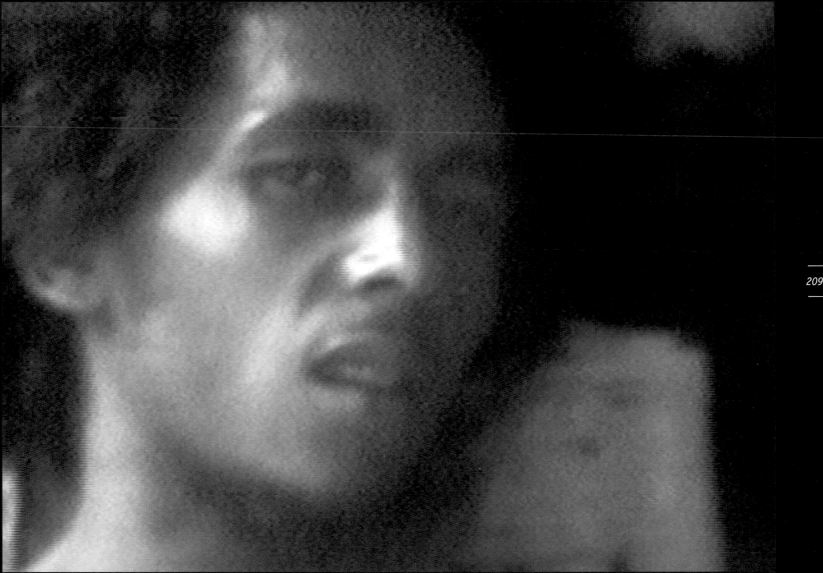

up. Peter's house was a step up from a shanty. It was one of those lower-lower-middle-class houses, all concrete. There were rows and rows of these houses, thoughtlessly built houses. I could never comprehend how they could build like that in Jamaica, a place of such beautiful indigenous woods. It was incongruous—a poet, Peter Tosh, living in one of them. Yvonne was there, light-skinned, maybe one-eighth or one-sixteenth black, green eyes. When I had first met her I had been shocked to see Peter, the most militant of the Wailers, with such an almost-white girl and so tiny, in contrast to his six-foot-four-inch frame. But you could see immediately that Peter was completely dedicated to her. He insisted that she go on the Wailers' *Burnin'* tour, and as I grew to know her, it was easy to understand his attachment. Though she was only nineteen, she was wise way beyond her years. "Wh'appen, Lee Jaffe?" Peter's voice bellowed as I got out of the car. I knew he was glad to see me, but tried not to show it. "No need to know wha' a gwan inna Babylon

right now. I&I fe do some work, seen? Jah work."

Yvonne was cooking some fish tea, which she offered me. "Wh'appen, can't get a spliff, mon?" I said to Peter.

"Yeah, mon, you know me have the best draw. Sit down, mon." And he pulled out a stick of herb. "Lamb's bread, mon, King's bread. I&I always have de best ilie." We ate and we smoked.

Peter had his cheap old acoustic guitar and played me songs he had written: "What You Gonna Do," "Burial," "Legalize It," "Why Must I Cry," and "Till the Well Runs Dry." I had my harmonicas and we jammed. Yvonne said, "Lee Jaffe mus' play harmonica on dis here album. People love your mouth organ, mon." The songs were powerful, sensitive, poetic songs of love, songs of revolution, multilayered songs, songs of illimitable power, songs of different colors, of different shades, timeless. And Peter's phrasing, so impeccable, so succinct, so Jamaican, so universal, so visceral, so vibrant. I knew I was in the presence of one of the great songwriters of our times. I also felt the intensity of his frustration, having

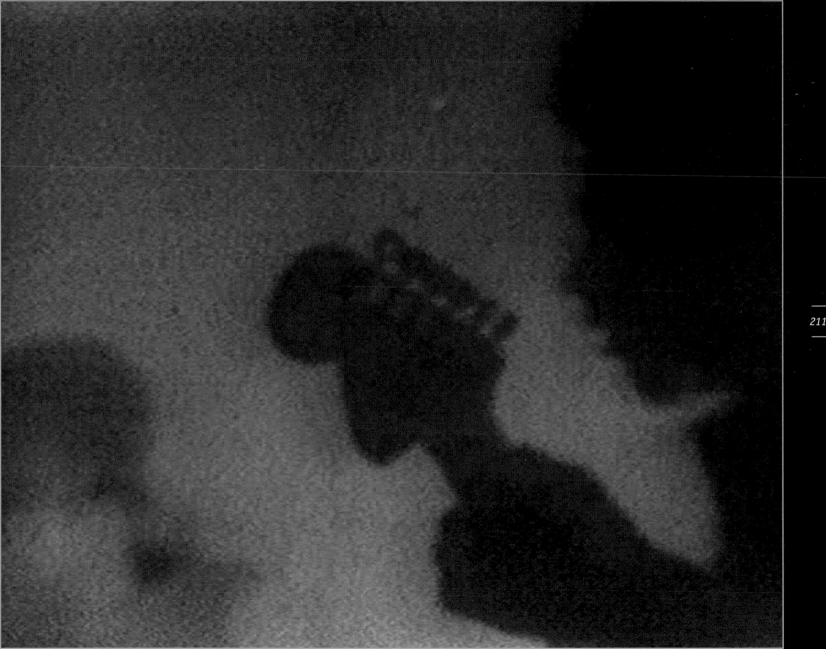

these incredible songs and not being able to get them out to the world. I felt honored to be in the presence of this great African prince, a spokesperson on the level of a Malcolm X who, for all his militancy, carried a vast amount of love and kindness in his heart. For all his advocacy of black power, he was a prudent anti-racist, and a fighter for the equality of all people. I knew little, however, of just how much tragedy was lurking. That Frowzer and Take Life would not live past twenty-five. That Carly, Carlton Barrett, the Wailers' drummer and brother of Aston, the Wailers' bass player, would be murdered. That Yvonne would soon die senselessly at nineteen. That Bob would be felled by cancer at the age of thirty-six. And that Peter, too, would be dead before his time, gunned down in his own home by a so-called friend.

Peter put aside his guitar and then suddenly he was gone, disappearing in a haze of smoke and song. Time had rushed by. It was after two AM when I went for my bag in the rental car. The silence was suddenly intense, still. The moon large, effervescent. Yvonne took me to a small room in the back of the house, a room with a bed and nothing else. Behind it was a back yard with a chicken coop. I slept a few hours. I could hear the rustling of the Jamaican dawn. Hens cackling, cocks crowing, porridge boiling, Irish mosh steaming. I could sense the ghosts of ex-slaves, the ones hung in Spanish Town Square. The captured runaways the colonialists chose to make a spectacle of. I could feel the heat beginning, the torment rising. Duppies, the island's ghosts, deranged, meandering through alleys and back streets, loitering invisible on street corners and gully banks—the souls of sufferers who could take no more—always present.

Soon we'd be recording the songs of protest. Peter and Yvonne had someone named Bullby that helped them around the yard. He had a hair lip and a club foot, and a big round head. He lisped when he spoke. I could hear him out back tossing feed to the fowl—they cackled. A maga dog barks, then howls. Another day in paradise.

I showered behind a plastic curtain. An all-concrete house with all-plastic curtains, furniture, accoutrements. Nothing made sense. Peter and Yvonne lived there, but it wasn't a home, just some temporary residence, some barely adequate retreat far enough from town to not be hassled. I loaded the tapes in Peter's car and he brought his guitar. It was an adventure driving with Peter, and he knew I hated it. There had been times before when I made him stop the car because he was so out of control.

I wasn't afraid of dying, but the thought of living with a mangled body held no appeal for me. He tempered his driving to suit me, but still it was manic, darting in and out of cars, tailgating

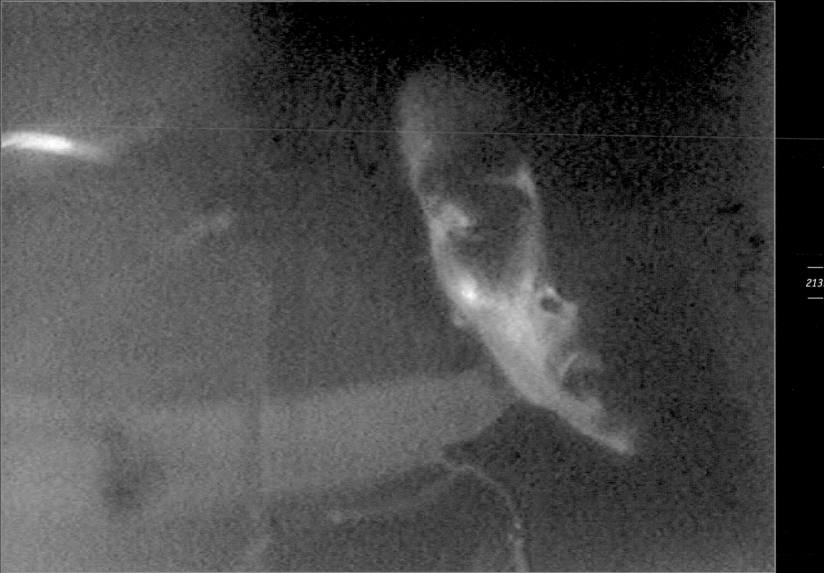

crazed taxi-men, passing oblivious truck drivers on the cause-way from Spanish Town to Kingston, where everyone envisioned themselves Formula One race drivers.

The screaming sun glistened off the water, then Kingston. Garbage heaps, dungle heaps, the lowest of the low picking through them. This was not garbage like in an American city. This was garbage that gulls and vultures had abandoned—rats no longer crawling, scurrying—only humans, the lowest on the ecological scale, were left to scavenge. These were the descendents of East Indian Untouchables, vanquished African tribes, and remnants of Arawak and Carib warriors who had been genocided to oblivion.

The temperature was rising in momentary increments; a bead of sweat trickled from my forehead, crawled down my neck, as we wove our way toward downtown around potholes, broken streets and bottles, the debris of total neglect, the stench of roads and alleys never cleaned, of hope abandoned.

We were downtown now and passed by Beeston Street, with the tiny Tuff Gong Records stand managed by Bob's wife Rita, a 6' x 6' deep storefront blaring old Wailers singles, next to a shop that sold fried sprat, a tiny sardine-like fish. There were people I recognized milling around the front of the store, and I nodded my head. "Hail, mon, hail, mon," the people acknowledged us. "Rastaman! Dreadlocks!" Peter stopped. Bucky Marshall bounded up to the car, engine still humming.

"Wha'ppen, Peter? A Lee Jah-free my bredrin." He grabbed my hand with his two and held it firmly. "A my spar dat," he beamed at Peter. It was an incredible acknowledgment. On the one hand, allowing no resentment toward Peter for being in the company of this white guy, and on the other, he himself this mythical ghetto hero racelessly embracing me. He had a large oval face atop a small lean frame, and with his head in the car, the thick scar that ran from the top of his skull in a more than semicircle past his jaw was overwhelming. His eyes had the intensity of a select fraternity who, consciously and with icy reason and extreme violence, have escorted multiple souls past the threshold of the hereafter.

Bucky was either a Robin Hood who defended the poor sufferers or an obdurate, remorseless killer—or both. I had met him on one of my first trips to Trench Town with Bob, and he had immediately accepted my presence. His vitriolic stare had bored precipitously deep into the chasm of my soul, and had come out, "Yes, you are with we—I man shall protect the I." Perhaps he felt that my just being there was some great act of courage, and was cause for respect—little did he know how naive I was. He always

Stills from a video shoot Leon Russell and I directed that was produced by Denny Cordell and Leon who were big Wailers
fans early on. Recorded with their state of the art mobile video truck, Capital Records studios in Los Angeles, 1973.

made a big show of how close we were, never asked me for anything, and it was Bucky's friendship that a year earlier had probably saved my life in Kingston Central. I was glad to see him. I was glad to see him on the street. Glad to see him alive and with his usual airy swagger, navigating through the geography of violence that the Kingston shanty towns had become.

Peter eased the car onto Orange Street and made a right turn to Treasure Isle. Treasure Isle was a proper record store, maybe about 20' x 20', with racks of albums and 45s, mostly Jamaican, with fluorescent lights and a real cash register. Above it was the Treasure Isle recording studio. We pulled the car up. We were ten minutes early for our sessions. There were three loud blasts. I looked at Peter. He didn't return my glare. My statement said, "What was that?" A pause and then Peter spoke. "It's not for I & I that we do these works, this is Jah's works, and when we perform Jah's works we can pass through the valley of death and fear no evil fi Jah protects I & I. For when I & I comes to know the fullness of Jah, then nothing can stop creation. Our music shall resound through all

nations and Babylon shall feel the full force of Jah's power and Babylon will come to its knees. Yes, Lee mon, nothing can stop I & I when we perform Jah's works."

Peter wasn't much older than I, only a few years, but at times, when he was prophesying, it seemed decades separated us—his spirituality so far more developed—and even though we served the same creator from the same Old Testament, even though I could trace my lineage to the same King Solomon, only in certain moments when blowing harmonica did I feel I could match the intensity of his resounding voice.

I strolled across the street to drink two jelly coconuts. The ital water made me feel alive again. Then a giant dark figure appeared in the doorway of Treasure Isle studio, imposing, larger than life, with ample girth expanding behind his belt buckle, gun handle peering out, enormous shoulders dominating the street, transforming it into an African version of a set from *The Wild Bunch* or *The Good, the Bad and the Ugly*. This was Duke Reid, whose studio and sound system produced countless Jamaican hits. Years later I was to discover that the holes in the ceiling of Treasure Isle were from gunshots from Duke's .38, fired

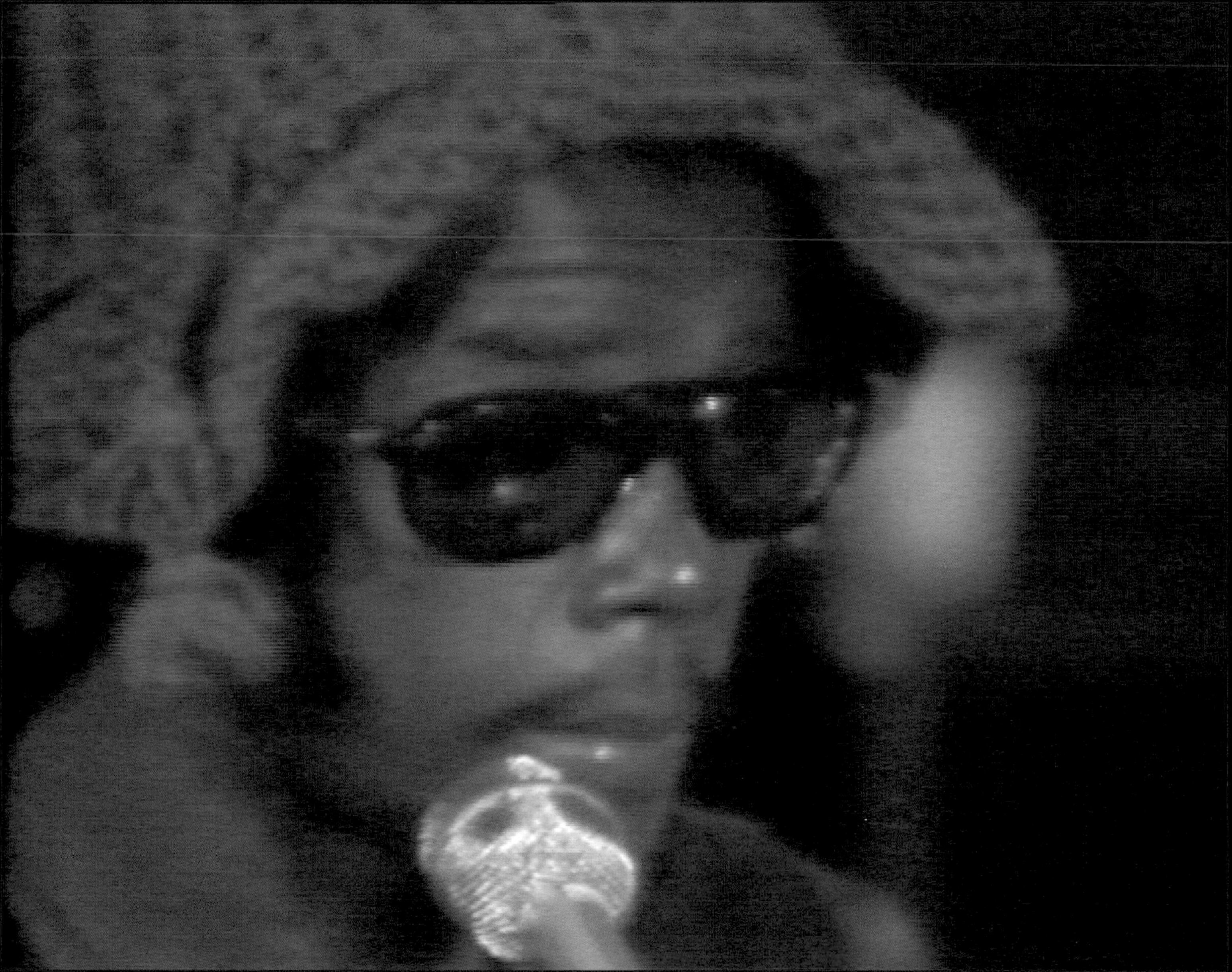

when singers would sing out of tune, or drummers would lose the beat. And my thoughts would return to that day, arriving outside the downtown Kingston studio for the first *Legalize It* sessions, and hearing those three loud blasts, and I'd realize it had probably been Duke letting off some steam.

I got the tapes and the guitar from the car, and Duke acknowledged Peter. "Wha'ppen Mr. Touch, you all right?"

"Not as good as you, sir."

Duke wore his big belly like a badge of success. We made our way up dim creaky stairs to the crowded fluorescent-lit studio, with its aging eight-track recorder. The house engineer was there. He had one eye and part of his ear had been chopped off. He had large creases in his forehead, deep creases. And I wondered, of the many classic records that had come out of this little hole in the wall, how many he had engineered.

He had a tiny, emaciated teenage assistant they called Skiddley. Peter gave me some herb to roll a spliff as Skiddley aligned the tape machine. Family Man and Carly sauntered in. There was a drum kit already in place. Fams had his Precision bass.

Peter wanted to use Family Man and Carly because he was so familiar with their playing, having played with them for so many years in the Wailers. I had my reservations, because I knew that if we wanted to tour with them, Bob would object. There were too many possibilities of scheduling conflicts. But I figured, for some of the album, why not? After all, it was Bob Marley and the Wailers. Peter had as much claim to that name, the Wailers, as anyone. But I knew eventually we would need a new bassist and drummer.

Carly got behind the drum kit and started getting some drum sounds. Family Man meticulously rolled his giant spliff. The air conditioning was blasting. I was aware of the sense of privilege the people who worked in the studio must have felt to be able to avoid the midday heat of Kingston, which was still called the King's town, even though Jamaica had received its so-called independence a decade earlier. Then Jumpy showed up, Tyrone Downey. American guitar player Al Anderson and I had convinced Bob to take Jumpy on the *Natty Dread* tour. We had seen Jumpy playing in hotels and although he was still a teenager, his playing was always transcendent. They called him Jumpy because his personality was so up, so bubbling with ideas, so uninhibited, and free to suggest things, even among players so much his senior.

Then, almost magically, they were all in the studio—Peter, Family, Carly, Al and Tyrone. I felt so high to be in that room, so honored to be a catalyst for what I knew would be a historic, timeless, classic session.

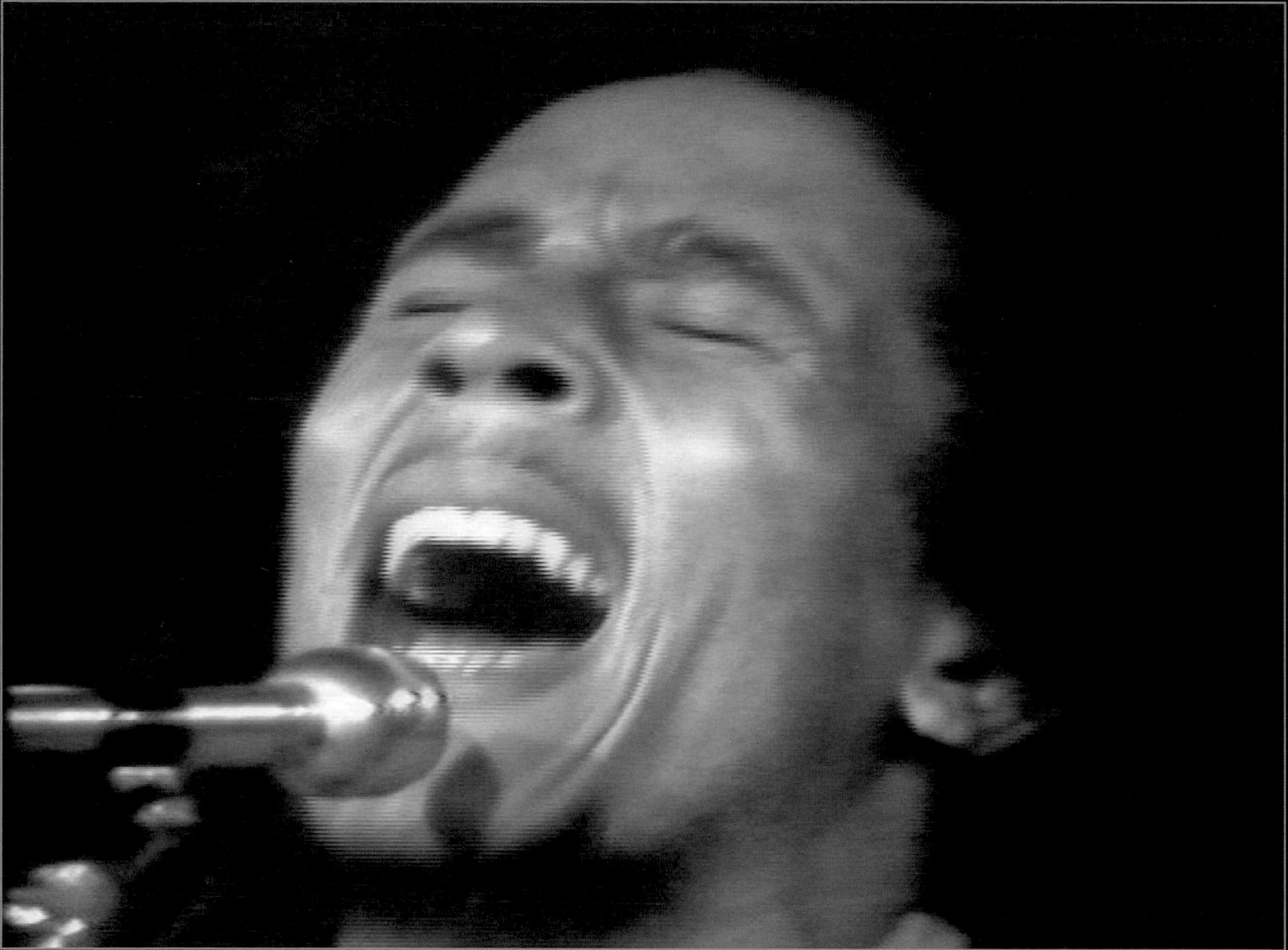

Lee Jaffe, Paris 1975.

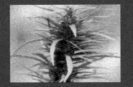

Acknowledgments

I would like to give special thanks to Chris Blackwell, whose strength courage and dedication enabled the Wailers to grow and flourish, for helping me to find a home away from home.

To Rita Marley for her brilliance and fortitude and for treating me like family during trying times.

To Bunny Wailer for his poetry, radicalism, and relentless sense of social justice.

To Esther Anderson for her feistiness and for introducing me to Jamaica.

To Perry Henzel for *The Harder They Come* and for his encouragement and kindness.

To Dickie Jobson for guiding my initial tour of Jamaica.

To Roger Steffens for helping me to navigate through some deep and turbulent waters.

To Geoff Gans for his sensitivity in creating a perfect rhythm and flow for the photographs, and for his exquisite layout and design of the book.

To Jim Mairs for his faith and keen editorial sense.

To Karen Grace for unfailing support and encouragement.

To Alex Masucci for his friendship and keen sense of humor.

To Rebecca Rogers for her discerning eye and tough criticism and long hours helping make the photos look right.

To my parents Harriette and Morris for their patience and understanding.

And to my children Aishlinn Kate 12, and Max Marley 15, and to all of their generation who are now discovering the music, for their constant inspiration.

223.

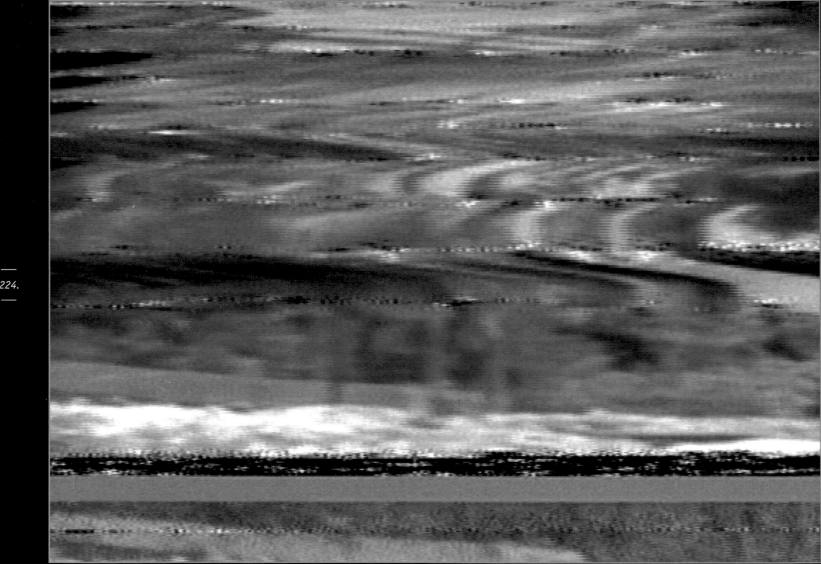